PRAISE FOR THIS BOOK'S CONTENT

Business challenges are unique for every community and country). I found all chapters appealing and useful, but Chapters 4 (Secrets Millionaires Use to Sell More) and 6 (Why Businesses Fail) stood out—*Moses K., IT officer.*

Your book was excellent.... it came at a time when I needed such information. When is your next publication? *David W. University Student*

I have only managed a quick perusal, but I can already see that it is going to really help me and my team. We are in the process of reevaluating our business strategy and processes in the day-to-day running of the company, so this lovely book comes in very handy. *Lorna S., Managing Partner, Law Firm.*

I would really like to appreciate you for the book. It is not only informative & educational; it is also so easy to read, especially for a not book-friendly person. I loved that real life examples are provided in addition to useful links and the sources of the information provided. For a person that is looking to start business, I found the chapter about "why businesses fail" totally on point. I also like the way the book was written, the humor and grammar; it gives me a feeling that I am getting advice from a professional over a chilly weekend. I could go all day explaining what I love about the book but I must thank you for the good work. Only God can pay you for your work. *David N. Al Ain, Abu Dhabi.*

The book is good. Thank you. I liked most the evaluation tools in the Appendices, so helpful. I am using it as my handbook now. *Rony M. Businessman.*

I loved the book. It is very informative. The kind of book one needs if one wants to make headway in business. *Regina O. Farmer.*

DEDICATIONS

To two remarkable USN Submariners who defined excellence in both leadership and life:

My father, MMCM Wallace Gerald Ingram Sr., was a man whose very presence commanded respect and whose integrity ran as deep as the oceans he sailed. In every step, in every word, he exemplified what leadership truly means. His empathy touched souls while his standards elevated everyone around him. I watched in awe as he moved through life with a cadence all his own, earning unconditional respect not by demand but by example. He showed me that true greatness lies not in the rank you wear but in the lives you touch and the standards you uphold.

ETCM Raymond Rudolph Kuhn Sr. (Life Mentor), Whose steady hand and compassionate heart guided me through life's most challenging seas. When the waters grew rough, his wisdom provided clarity, his patience offered direction, and his understanding lit the way forward. **TI**

To all those entrepreneurs who strive to succeed despite all the odds stacked against you. **DW.**

TABLE OF CONTENTS

Praise for this book's content i
Dedications ii
What is our story? 1
How to read this book 5

Book I - Sea Faring Legs 7

Chapter 1	The Sounds of Dive, Dive, Dive	9
Chapter 2	Taming The Money Monster	21
Chapter 3	Navigating the Seas of Change	41
Chapter 4	Secrets Millionaires Use to Sell More	55
Chapter 5	Are You Ready To Take The Helm?	67
Chapter 6	Why Businesses Fail	81
Chapter 7	Navigating the Seas to Entrepreneurship	89
Chapter 8	How To Get All The Funding You Need	109
Chapter 9	The Silent Shift - Turning Inward	117
Chapter 10	Ensuring Your Business Lasts For 100+ Years	129
	How The Story Ends	139

Book II - Appendices & Supplementary Material 145

Appendix I	Sample Business TOOLKITS	147
Appendix II	Sample internal control program	155
Appendix III	Legal Checklist for starting a business	173
Appendix IV	Import/Export Checklist for US Entrepreneurs	179
Appendix V	Common FAQs that Entrepreneurs Ask	185

Acknowledgements and Contact 191
About The Authors 195

WHAT IS OUR STORY?

Welcome aboard! In the world of business, success requires more than ambition. It demands discipline, strategy, and a solid understanding of finances. This book provides just that. *"Depth & Dividends: A USN Submariner to CEO and a CPA Share 10 Strategic Lessons for Thriving in Global Business Environments. "* is a comprehensive guide—or compass—that combines the strategic mindset of a Navy Veteran to CEO (me, Terry Ingram) with the financial expertise of a CPA who worked with global accounting firms and is an ex-audit partner (yours truly, D.E. Wasake). It is designed to help entrepreneurs and business leaders thrive in a challenging global business environment.

The book blends real-world entrepreneurial experience with professional insight to provide readers with actionable insights, proven strategies, and practical tools for immediate deployment in your business operations, whether you are charting your startup's maiden voyage or navigating an established enterprise through challenging waters. You will especially love the 15+ toolkit items, templates, and guides in Appendix *I-V* to help ensure your success. But what led us to this point? Here are snippets of our story.

Dive, Dive, Dive (by T.I)

The cold metal of the submarine's hatch felt like ice against my palm as I descended into the belly of what we called "The Boat." The air thickened with each step down the ladder—a mixture of sweat, machinery, and anticipation. This was it—my first dive as an unqualified submariner. The weight of responsibility settled on my shoulders, heavier than the pressures that would soon surround us.

Growing up in a military family of six, with a father who served 34 years in the U.S. submarine service and a godfather with over 40 years under his belt, I thought I knew what to expect. After all, I had spent weeks on the boat during my father's duty, walking around in awe of my surroundings. But I was naively unaware of what it truly meant to be in a tube that dived beneath the ocean's surface. Many years later, as I will share in the book, I realized that the most valuable cargo I carried from my naval career was not in my sea bag. It was the intangible yet invaluable lessons, experiences, and mindset that continue to guide me as I navigate the ever-changing currents of entrepreneurship. And for that, I will be eternally grateful to the silent service and the extraordinary individuals with whom I had the honor to serve. In this book, I have included several lessons from the turns and twists that have been my journey as an entrepreneur, and I will help you learn how to slay that Leviathan monster of the sea called business. I will share with you lessons, anecdotes, and hopefully sage advice on the following:

1. Why the only thing we can control is what is within these four walls – meaning learning how to navigate your own fears, which many today call "imposter syndrome."
2. How to handle uncertainty and navigate the seas of change including how after I left the Navy service, I told one guy "See you next Tuesday" even after he had sternly warned me to NEVER turn up again at his office.
3. What it means when you need to take the helm of leadership (I hope you don't mind all the sea-related puns).
4. How to take the 1st steps of transition from employee to entrepreneur
5. Ensuring the journey doesn't consume you and your family.

See you next Tuesday – Landlubber! *Terry J. Ingram (T. I.)*

The Chook Chook Train (By D.W)

Accountants are sometimes referred to in a "tongue-in-cheek" fashion as boring, so I will not make your will to live any worse with stories about how I became a UK CPA (Chartered Accountant or FCCA) or how, 20 years later, with my gray hairs threatening to take over my head, I successfully completed my US CPA exams in 8 months with first-time passes. I am, however, reminded of the story of a famous Bahamian poet friend, Obediah. He once jokingly mocked me, asking, "What good could possibly come out of double entry?" In reply, I said (poetically, of course): *The Caribbean express, On and on he goes, Like the chook chook train, Trainloads of words, never broken, never derailed.*

This book really started on the day when, straight out of University, I borrowed my big brother's ill-fitting suit (a green one at that), jumped onto a *boda boda* motorbike in my native Uganda, and headed off to make a presentation to the son-in-law of the Ugandan president.

WHAT I DIDN'T TELL him is that the internal control concepts I was about to discuss were coming straight from my university "auditing 101" notes - concepts I had no real experience in. WHAT I DIDN'T KNOW THOUGH was that the notes were so effective that the company eventually paid me my first check – thanks business school. Several years later, I am wiser (I hope) and have real practical experience. I have also been lucky to see first-hand how big and successful companies are run. My largest client had $1.3 trillion in Assets Under Management.

Much of the information in this book is born out of the "nagging" need to share and change the USA and the world, and I am thankful for Terry, my business partner at Ingram Advisory Group, with whom I get to be a world changer. Many people mock us business advisors, saying, "Those who cannot do consult," or "It is a waste of time and money," but this cannot be further from the truth.

I have heard a good saying: *"If you think hiring a professional is expensive, try an amateur."*.... I believe it is important to get the best advice, and this book combines that advice – Terry's entrepreneurial journey combined with my professional precision in dissecting business challenges – and now that is what you describe as a Torpedo to success. What are you waiting for? Get onto the Chook Chook train!

D. E. Wasake (DW)

HOW TO READ THIS BOOK

When you read this book, you will find narrative sections where I, Terry, give you entrepreneurial "real life" examples, including my journey from a US Submariner to a CEO. Dickson, my CPA partner, will zoom into specific aspects of my story to give you a principle, research, or similar professional insight so that as you read along, you get both the bones (framework) and the muscle (experience). This means, as with any book, the best way to read this book is sequentially. However, we understand that busy entrepreneurs may not have time to read it cover to cover or may prefer to focus on specific topics.

We considered this when writing the book and designed each chapter to stand alone. This means you can read any chapter without needing to read others first. If you prefer to read this book in parts, we suggest reading the following chapters:

Chapter 1: The Sounds of Dive, Dive Dive

Chapter 2: Taming the Money Monster

Chapter 3: Navigating the Seas of Change

Chapter 4: Secrets Millionaires Use To Sell More

Chapter 6: Why Businesses Fail.

Chapter 7: Navigating the Seas of Entrepreneurship

The appendices include helpful templates and checklists, and we specifically include two appendices for thriving in the complex U.S. business environment. Be sure not to skip them!

Let's go into the deep sea!

BOOK I
SEA FARING LEGS

CHAPTER 1
THE SOUNDS OF DIVE, DIVE, DIVE

The cold metal of the submarine's hatch felt like ice against my palm as I descended into the belly of what we called "The Boat." The air thickened with each step down the ladder—a mixture of sweat, machinery, and anticipation. This was it—my first dive as an unqualified submariner. The weight of responsibility settled on my shoulders, heavier than the pressures that would soon surround us.

Growing up in a military family of six, with a father who served 34 years in the U.S. submarine service and a godfather with over 40 years under his belt, I thought I knew what to expect. After all, I had spent weeks on the boat during my father's duty, walking around in awe of my surroundings. But I was naively unaware of what it truly meant to be in a tube that dived beneath the ocean's surface. They had instilled in me an unrelenting vision that anything was possible. But nothing truly prepares you for that moment when theory becomes a reality, when the comforting presence of the surface world disappears, and you're left with only your training, your crew, and the unforgiving sea.

As the klaxon sounded and the order to dive echoed through the narrow passageways, a knot formed in my stomach. My hands moved automatically, performing the tasks I had drilled countless times, but my mind raced. Could I really do this? What if I made a mistake? There was no way out. The lives of every man on board depended on each of us performing our duties flawlessly.

Depth and dividends

I glanced around at my shipmates, their faces a mixture of concentration and calm. They trusted me, just as I trusted them. In this metal tube beneath the waves, trust wasn't just important—it was everything. We were each other's lifelines, bound by duty, training, and the shared understanding that our lives depended on one another.

This was the first reality check that I had no choice; my shipmates were relying on me.

The captain's voice crackled over the intercom, steady and confident. His words carried the weight of command but also conveyed faith in his crew. He demanded the highest standards from each of us, a level that felt overwhelming in its intensity. Yet, his tone also carried encouragement—he believed in us, in me.

As we descended deeper, the pressure outside the hull increased with each meter, and I felt a similar tension building inside me. The academic struggles of my past flashed through my mind. I had always found more success with my hands than with books, struggling through submarine school, but my command master chief always said my time to shine would come, proving time and again that the combination of practical skills and determination could overcome any obstacle. Now, faced with the complex systems and split-second decisions required to keep us all alive, I questioned whether that would be enough.

But then I remembered my mother's unwavering belief in me, her determination to see me succeed despite any odds. I thought of my father and godfather and the legacy they had built in the silent service. Their stories of perseverance, of overcoming fears and insecurities, echoed in my mind." No was not in my vocabulary, driven by the belief they too had in my understanding the responsibilities that I would now need to live and accept."

As the depth gauge showed our descent leveling off, a calm settled over me. I realized this wasn't just about individual capability—it was about teamwork in its purest form. My shipmates moved with practiced efficiency, each

Chapter 1: The Sounds of Dive, Dive, Dive

performing their role while remaining ready to support one another at a moment's notice. This was self-preservation at its most fundamental, transformed into a collective effort that transcended personal fears.

The dive continued, hours stretching into days and a timeless expanse of focused activity. With each passing moment, my confidence grew. Not because my fears disappeared but because I understood that they were a natural part of the process. Everyone around me, even the most seasoned veterans, felt the weight of our responsibility. The difference was in how we channeled that pressure into performance.

As we finally surfaced for my first time hearing "Surface, Surface Surface," breaching the waves to rejoin the world above, I felt changed. The insecurities were still there, but they no longer dominated my thoughts. Instead, I felt a deep sense of accomplishment and belonging. I had taken the plunge, faced my fears, and emerged stronger for it after over two months submerged.

Yet, this was just the beginning. The journey to becoming a fully qualified submariner was a rigorous process that lay ahead. The fear of letting my father down, of not qualifying, loomed large in my mind. It was a fear that would drive me, push me to my limits, and ultimately shape me into the person I would become.

What today I look back on was sheer drive, a team of shipmates from the Commanding Officer to the lowest ranking man onboard we are going to make you who you indeed are a submariner; their unwavering push, pull, and commitment gave me the unwavering desire to succeed "TEAM WORK" at its best.

The moment after my NAVY enlistment – with my mother watching on and shaking my father's hand (he rests in Arlington National Cemetery).

The qualification process was intense, starting with schooling prior to joining the boat. Every day was a test, every moment an opportunity to prove myself or fall short. The weight of the insignia - that small piece of metal that represented so much - felt heavier with each passing day. It wasn't just a symbol of achievement; it was a badge of honor worn by very few in the world, a testament to the rigorous standards and unforgiving nature of submarine service.

I remember sitting in the mess, the submarine's version of a living room. It was where we ate, talked, watched movies, and bonded as a family. In those moments, surrounded by my shipmates, I often felt like an entrepreneur just starting - not always understanding what was happening around me but forcing myself to push through, to learn, to adapt.

Time became an abstract concept underwater. Without the sun to mark the passing of days, our lives were dictated by the artificial lighting within the submarine. This disorientation, this detachment from the everyday rhythms of life, taught me a valuable lesson that would serve me well in my future entrepreneurial endeavors: success isn't always measured by traditional markers. Just as we had to find our way of marking time and progress underwater, in the business world, I would learn that true success is measured not by arbitrary standards but by the real impact we have and the value we create.

Parallels between submarine life and entrepreneurship

There are several parallels between submarine life and entrepreneurship, as I will show you, but for me, the parallels became even more evident when I thought about, for example, the area of customer feedback.

On a submarine, your performance isn't judged by platitudes or empty praise. Your shipmates' lives depend on your competence, and they won't hesitate to let you know when you're falling short. This brutal honesty and commitment to continuous improvement is mirrored in the business world. As I later learned, customers don't praise you just because you're trying hard. They challenge you and push you to be better, and it's this constant feedback - both positive and negative - that drives actual growth and innovation.

As I progressed through my qualification process, facing numerous tests and challenges, I began to understand that the fear of failure, the fear of letting my father down, wasn't a weakness. It was a driving force, pushing me to excel, dig deeper, and find reserves of strength and determination I didn't know I possessed. This lesson would prove invaluable in my future entrepreneurial journey, where the fear of failure often coexists with the drive to succeed.

The day of my final qualification board remains etched in my memory. I was sitting before a panel of senior officers, senior enlisted, and yes, a junior peer, their faces impassive as they fired question after question at me for over six hours or more. It seemed never-ending. I felt the weight of everything I had worked for bearing down on me. It wasn't just about technical knowledge -

though that was crucial. It was about demonstrating that I had internalized the submarine ethos and that I understood the gravity of the responsibility I was asked to take on. That every single man onboard would forever look at me differently and expect me to never waver in the good of the crew.

As the board concluded and I waited for their decision, I reflected on the journey that had brought me to this point. The long hours of study, the countless drills, the moments of doubt and triumph all led to this moment. When the announcement came that I had passed and was now qualified to wear the submarine insignia, the sense of achievement was overwhelming. But more than that, I felt a profound sense of belonging, having earned my place in this elite community.

The weight of the submarine insignia pinned to my chest signified more than just the culmination of grueling training or the right to serve aboard the Navy's silent sentinels. Those dolphins became an anchor, tethering me to a set of principles and experiences that would shape the course of my life long after I left the sea behind.

In the cramped confines of a submarine, where every cubic inch is accounted for, and every crew member's role is critical, I learned the true meaning of efficiency and teamwork. The constant hum of machinery, the disciplined rhythm of watch rotations, and the knowledge that our lives depended on each other's competence - these elements forged a mindset that would prove invaluable in the civilian world.

As I hung up my sea bag for the last time, my fingers tracing the worn fabric that had accompanied me to the ocean's depths, I realized the Navy had equipped me with far more than technical prowess. The relentless pace of submarine operations, the unwavering standards that governed every action, and the necessity of performing flawlessly under immense pressure - these were the very qualities that would fuel my journey as an entrepreneur.

The transition from sailor to civilian was not without its challenges. The structured environment of military life gave way to the uncertain seas of the business world. Yet, I found myself surprisingly well-prepared for this new adventure. The problem-solving skills honed during equipment failures at crush depth translated seamlessly into troubleshooting business challenges.

The strategic thinking required for mission planning became the foundation for crafting market strategies and business models.

In the submarine service, we lived by the motto "improvise, adapt, and overcome." Little did I know how prophetic those words would be for my entrepreneurial journey. The resilience built during long deployments cut off from the world above became the strength to weather market downturns and setbacks. The innovation required to make do with limited resources underwater became the creativity to bootstrap a startup with minimal capital.

Navigating the turbulent waters of civilian business

The lessons learned hundreds of feet below the surface proved invaluable in navigating the often-turbulent waters of civilian business. The teamwork vital to submarine operations translated seamlessly into building and leading companies. The attention to detail required to operate complex systems became the keen eye for spotting market opportunities and refining product designs.

Perhaps most importantly, my time in the silent service instilled a sense of mission and purpose that extended far beyond personal gain. Just as we had served a cause greater than ourselves beneath the waves, I found myself driven to create businesses that not only succeeded financially but also contributed positively to society.

In earning those dolphins, I had unknowingly charted a course to entrepreneurship. With its rigorous academic, practical, and leadership requirements, the submarine qualification process had been more than a test of naval competence. It was, in retrospect, a comprehensive preparation for the challenges of building and running successful enterprises.

Though I no longer wear the uniform, the spirit of innovation, resilience, and excellence instilled during those years continues to propel me forward. The pressure hull of a submarine and the boardroom of a startup may seem worlds apart, but the core principles of leadership, teamwork, and perseverance remain the same.

One lesson you can take from the military to apply to your business as you develop your mission and purpose is the concept of commander's intent.

Commander's Intent

Commander's intent is a powerful concept used in military operations to convey the purpose of a mission, allowing teams to understand the desired end state even if the original plan changes. This principle fosters initiative and adaptability by ensuring everyone understands the overarching goal, which is crucial in dynamic environments.

As an example, if the commander's intent was to go to enemy territory and grab the flag, knowing this, even if the commander didn't tell you about the minefields along the way, will give you a clear purpose and help you to plan how to get there and to innovate in case the original plan changes, while sticking to the mission.

To apply this to a business, you must define a clear mission and purpose. Outline the overarching goals and desired outcomes so the team can make decisions aligned with the company's vision, even if conditions change. For example, in setting up a startup, Commander's Intent ensures that each member understands the core mission, such as solving a specific customer problem. This helps them adapt if initial plans need to shift.

Another related military strategy you can employ is Mission Command. This strategy emphasizes empowering subordinates to make decisions within the framework of a clear mission. Defining a clear mission and vision in business allows team members to act autonomously while aligning with the company's objectives. You recall I told you how critical a team was in my first dive experience; it is critical in business, too.

As I close this chapter of my journey, I realize that my time beneath the waves prepared me not just for a career but for a lifetime of charting new territories in the business world. The submarine insignia may no longer adorn my chest, but its imprint on my character, ethos, and approach to life's challenges remains indelible. It stands as a constant reminder that with the right mindset, training, and determination, we can navigate any depth, weather any storm, and emerge stronger on the other side.

Ultimately, the most valuable cargo from my naval career wasn't in my sea bag. It was the intangible yet invaluable lessons, experiences, and mindset that continue to guide me as I navigate the ever-changing currents of entrepreneurship. And for that, I will be eternally grateful to the silent service and the extraordinary individuals with whom I had the honor to serve.

Lesson summary: What This Means for You in Business

- **Preparedness is Key**: Just as a submarine must be ready for unexpected challenges, a business must prepare for economic uncertainties and market shifts.
- **Trust Your Crew**: Effective delegation and trust in your team are essential for efficient operations.
- **Discipline Equals Freedom**: Strong routines and processes create the freedom to innovate and grow.

The self-discipline homed in the ocean's depths to control anxiety and manage uncontrollable factors became a cornerstone of my business acumen. It accelerated my ability to communicate with clarity and maintain calm during the most challenging times in my career. We all have triggers influencing our deepest concerns, but I was fortunate to confront mine early on. These lessons taught me a profound truth: there are no problems, only solutions. "No" is not in our vocabulary; instead, we say "yes" to creating a path forward.

As you reflect on your own business experiences, consider the personal challenges you've faced and overcome. What obstacles have you stabilized that could, in turn, pave a more profound path for you mentally? How have these experiences prepared you to tackle the most profound challenges in business? Remember, the ability to remain composed and solution-oriented in the face of adversity is a skill that transcends industries and roles.

Someone once told me, "The only thing we can control is what's inside these four walls." Years later, I still find this advice to be unequivocally accurate. So, I ask you: How are you managing what is within your four walls of business? Are you fostering an environment of innovation, resilience, and unwavering determination? Are you building a team that, like a submarine crew, can operate seamlessly under pressure?

In my journey, I've learned the invaluable lesson of having an advisor close to you. As I did, having strong leadership to guide me through challenges proved crucial. Remember, one should never be ashamed to seek guidance, no matter how large or small your organization is. We all strive to bring more decisive leadership and confidence to our team, and sometimes, that means recognizing when we need external perspective and support.

If you want an external perspective, one tool you will need for your toolkit is a market research template to help you, and I have included one to give you a starting point. It is in *Appendix 1*.

Why do you need to do market research? A strong mission keeps your business focused, while a compelling vision gives it a future. Market research helps to put flesh into the mission to ensure you survive.

Otherwise, it is ultimately the responsibility of every leader to prove to oneself and their team that they can rise above insecurities and self-doubt by bringing in support without feeling ashamed. At the end of the day, your actions will also relay to your team that they, too, should reach out without stigma or embarrassment.

Dive deep into your own experiences. Examine the lessons you've learned from your personal and professional challenges. How can you leverage these insights to navigate the often turbulent waters of entrepreneurship? How can you apply the commander's intent principle?

Remember, the most valuable assets in business are frequently not tangible – they're the mental fortitude, adaptability, and problem-solving skills you've developed throughout your journey. By harnessing these qualities and surrounding yourself with wise counsel, you'll be well-equipped to chart a course through any business challenge, no matter how daunting it may seem. As you move forward in your entrepreneurial journey, remember that true strength often lies in knowing when to seek advice and how to build a support network. By doing so, you not only strengthen your leadership but also create an environment where your entire team can thrive with confidence.

In conclusion, success is built on preparation, trust, and discipline, whether in the depths of the ocean or the business world. Dive deep, stay focused, and lead with confidence.

Toolkit items you need at this stage (See Appendix I)

1. Market research template.
2. Team motivation plan
3. Risk assessment template

CHAPTER 2
TAMING THE MONEY MONSTER

I want to pick up on a few key phrases Terry spoke about in the initial chapter. He, for example, said:

> *"But nothing truly prepares you for that moment when theory becomes a reality, when the comforting presence of the surface world disappears, and you're left with only your training, your crew, and the unforgiving sea."*

You are going to face monsters in the unforgiving sea – perhaps Leviathan, Moby Dick, or the Great White Shark. What do you do to handle the inner and outer darkness?

He then shared something else, he said:

> *"The self-discipline homed in the ocean's depths to control anxiety and manage uncontrollable factors became a cornerstone of my business acumen."*

This means that when you face sea monsters, it is self-discipline that allows you to tame those thrashing beasts of old.

One of the first monsters you need to learn to tame in your personal life (and hence personal fears) is the money monster – because if you cannot tame it in your personal life, it spills over into business life.

I have seen many clients whose personal indiscipline in money matters has slipped into the business. Just like they never had the discipline to review

Depth and dividends

personal bank statements, they often didn't pay attention to the business books and soon were borrowing without regard to the high-interest cost. These clients didn't understand or forgot the discipline to know that every little penny adds up!

Before I show you how to tame the monster, if you really want to know some more about me and the chook chook train journey I took from my original home to here in the US, the first thing you are probably wanting to know is where I was born and all that *the Catcher in the Rye* reading I had to do.

The second thing is you probably want to know about my parents and all. I am not going to go into too much personal detail about me or about my parents; I leave that for Terry. I am his silent wingman analyzing behind the curtain, so you can call me Ishmael. You can call me One Patch Eye Hooker (OPEH), my childhood pirate name, heck you can even call me Mr. Chook Chook Train but probably don't call me King Kunta [Kinte], like them nasty folk I met while in the Caribbean, that wouldn't be so nice.

Suffice it to say, however, that the money monster (or lack of money) was always with me, especially after Ol' Daddy man (before he went up to that heavenly place) left Mum and all of us seven kids to fend for ourselves. That was indeed the worst of times, and so it was the 1st monster I had to conquer before I could fully become who I am, and so I know what principles to follow if you need to tame this leviathan monster thrashing about by the rivers of Babylon. I especially learned to tame it through a hard lesson on living beyond your means, so let me share that tale a little bit before I give you the seven money principles you need.

In 20XX, I was an FCCA in the making. This FCCA means Fellow of the Association of Chartered Certified Accountants, and I now hold the title. First, you become a member after harrowing exams and "sweating plasma" from studying day and night to qualify. Then, after five years of membership, you become a fellow. In total, this takes, say, 10 years. Fellowship is, therefore, a big deal.

Chapter 2: Taming The Money Monster

A fundamental principle of being an FCCA or a CPA here in the US is that you should never declare bankruptcy. If you do that, you can kiss goodbye to your qualifications. For example, how can the public trust you to handle their money if you can't handle your own?

Was this the point Cedric M, FCCA, was trying to tell me when he called me on the phone? Said Cedric M, FCCA and manager at the global accountancy firm where I was a trainee: *"Sort this guy out, and in the process, sort your life out."*

The guy in question was elderly Mr. Azalia L, a second-hand clothes dealer from Nasser Road, Kampala. The name "Nasser Road" in Ugandan circles evokes unease, as it is known to be a place where anything can be forged. He, therefore, might as well have been called "conman." Mr. Azalia was, however, no conman; I was the conman, so to speak.

A few months before Cedric M, FCCA's terse call, this upstanding man had sold me my first car, a second-hand 4WD SUV, where colleagues at my pay grade were driving more modest fuel-efficient vehicles.

Mr. Azalia accepted partial payment based on a gentleman's agreement (a handshake). After all, I was an accountant—those stalwart defenders of morality and honesty in a society falling apart at the seams. I was even the quintessential good-mannered: "It's a napkin, not a serviette, Mr. A."

Soon after the sale, Mr. Azalia had no idea I was coming apart at the seams. Actually, the car he sold me was draining my bank account.

The cost of maintaining it, let alone filling up the tank, was beyond my pay grade. That I was unaware of this was in no way his fault. Before beginning any major endeavor, let alone buying a car for the first time, a sane person should do their homework. I went ahead despite my older brother's repeated warnings.

This was the brother who had lent me my first suit, as I narrated in the introduction. I decided to buy the car partly because I wanted to feel cool driving around in a flashy vehicle. His pleas were brushed aside when he warned me about the cost of gas and car repairs. He implored me that it was not true that every car I saw on the road was a maroon 4WD, like the one I wanted.

No, what I was seeing at work was "Reticular Activating System (RAS)." A set of neurons being sent from my eyes to the brain to tell me what I wanted to see, in other words, here was the ancient principle at work: "You only see what you want to see."

By the time Mr. Azalia turned up at our office reception yelling: "WHERE IS THIS WASAKE MAN? I WANT MY MONEY!" he had figured out what many of the informal sector knew about some of us in our corporate offices, with our suits and ties. We were: *"heads high, pockets dry."*

I survived the embarrassment of "Azalia, the villager oaf" only because I was not in the office at the time of his unceremonious visit. I was, however, on the other end of the phone line when Cedric M, FCCA, delivered his verdict and insight, which can be interpreted this way: "In sorting out your money, you will sort out your life."

What lessons could you learn about money from a guy who once had to dodge Azalia, the second-hand clothes dealer?

Chapter 2: Taming The Money Monster

A lesson in giving money away from a billionaire

Bill Gates, the one some call the "Anti-Christ," can teach you an unusual lesson about money and how to tame the monster –by giving it away. So, some time back, when Gates was the wealthiest man in the world, his position as the world's richest man was threatened by the likes of Carlos Slim Hemu and family.

From his friend, Warren Buffet, his Bill & Melinda Gates Foundation received a financial boost, and combined with his paying more attention to it from 2008, it grew. Now, when I talk about growing, I am not talking about small

Depth and dividends

bucks. This foundation is huge. It had over $75 billion in assets (2023). At the time of writing, it was one of the largest private foundations in the world.

Now, here is the fun part! It seems that the more Gates gives his money away through this foundation (e.g., for AIDS, Tuberculosis, Polio, and other charity ventures), the wealthier he seems to get. In the last few years, his wealth seems to have not been increasing steadily in a growth curve but rather "jumping."

As an example, in 2008, his wealth grew by 4%. This is the year he left Microsoft to spend more time on the foundation. His wealth fell sharply the following year, mainly due to the 2008 financial crisis. Still, it quickly recovered and by 2010 had increased by 33% and continued to do so over the next few years. Even as he added much money to the foundation, his wealth was growing even more than before 2008, the seminal year. His wealth had previously grown by about 6% per year, but by 2017, it was averaging 15% yearly!

I realized that there might be something beyond Mr. Gates that is at work and not dark forces or even natural financial market forces but good forces.

I realized his wealth seemed to grow in response to ancient principles or universal laws on giving. It is as if when some wealth flies out through the window (to his foundation), more wealth comes crashing through the door and ventilators, and he has no standing room in his house (or is it a mansion?).

The first lesson I, therefore, have learned about taming the money monster is to give it away, and I thank "the Anti-Christ," Mr. Gates, for that.

Now let me tell you another secret that this man, Mr. Gates, knows. Giving money away is great, but there is a connection between maintaining sustainable, long-lasting wealth that you can give away and the type of friends you keep.

A fascinating trend stood out when I obtained a summary of those billionaires who had been on Forbes Magazine's top 10 list for 20 years from 2000 – 2019. Only two people have been on this list for the entire 20-year period. Those two people are Bill Gates and Warren Buffet. They also happen to be best friends.

You likely know this part of the story, but here goes. Introduced to one another by Bill Gates' mother in 1991, the two men didn't initially want to meet each other, but over the years, they have become so close that Gates says Buffet is one of the few people on his speed dial. It means your closest friends might initially look like the devil but turn out to be an angel of light.

If you do not like my references to Mr. Gates, here is one more proof of the validity of this nugget of wisdom for you. Per my review, the number 3 man on the list was Larry Ellison. One of his best friends was Steve Jobs (RIP), the co-founder of Apple. Yes, that Apple company, the maker of "i" everythin': iPhone, iPad, iOS, iTunes, and iCloud.

It seems then that friends sharpen other friends to tame the money monster. Who will be your Buffet, your Jobs?

Why do most of us struggle to manage money?

You are not alone if you are struggling with taming the money monster. Why do most adults struggle to manage money? Here are some statistics from the US to help you put these frightening money realities into perspective:

- 12% of U.S. adults reported having no savings at all as of May 2023.
- 13% of Americans over 60 have no retirement savings, with younger demographics facing even higher percentages; for instance, 42% of individuals aged 18-29 have no retirement savings.
- A survey found that 49% of U.S. adults have either less or no emergency savings.

Unless something is done, 49% of the population of the U.S., which is generally considered to be a wealthy country, is on the brink of poverty. Let me explain this another way.

The average weekly expenditure in the U.S. is about $1,486 (2023). Should a disaster or emergency occur – for example, sickness, a family death, or a major asset breakdown (e.g., car, house repairs, etc.), about half of this population would not survive more than a month without depending on the state (e.g., social security) or on someone else (e.g., family, charities, lenders, or friends) because their savings would not be enough to help them survive the disaster/emergency, especially if it meant they could also no longer work, for example, during a long-term illness.

So why aren't we saving? There are various reasons, but for example:

- 60% say they live from paycheck to paycheck.
- Only 34% can answer basic financial literacy questions – meaning they lack knowledge of budgeting, investing, and saving effectively.

This means that the lack of savings is a combination of having "little money" and just failing to plan. If this is the situation in the "developed world," what about the "developing world" where, amongst many African nations, there is no government social security program to fall back on?

This financial stress is a leading cause of suicide. It contributes to families falling into poverty, e.g., when a medical emergency comes and leads to family breakups due to conflicts over money or lack thereof, such as what happened to my family.

Based on this background, what are the seven money principles I have studied that you should learn? How did I start taming this beast?

Seven (7) money principles you could learn from

Money principle #1: Write things down (budgeting)

I really started taming the money beast when I started applying this principle, which is really the beginning of financial literacy. It works like this: when you write down the money coming in and going out, such a document is called a "budget."

If you are, for example, in January and can prepare a budget for the entire year up to the end of December, then you are doing "forecasting" or "financial planning."

Making a budget like this can shed light on the months in which you may need to put in extra effort, such as when unexpected costs arise. It can conversely show you the months in which you may be able to save more money, such as when you have paid off a debt. It is, however, easy to misjudge your financial situation if you don't keep track of your transactions on paper, a spreadsheet, or an APP.

As I will explain in more detail in the principles that follow, the primary function of a budget is to reveal the amount of money that can be set aside for savings and investment.

Below is an example budget to help illustrate this important principle.

Table 1: An illustrative budget

Month/Item	January	February	March
Money in (e.g., *from business*)	$1,000	$1,000	$1,000
Add **extra money in** (e.g., *selling Lobsters*)	$0	$0	$500
Total money in	$1,000	$1,000	$1,500
Minus: **Money out** (e.g., *food, water*)	($500)	($500)	($500)
Balance to save	$500	$500	$1,000

According to the above budget, if your income is $1,000 monthly (January, February, and March) and you spend the same amount each month ($500),

Depth and dividends

you should have $500 remaining in your account at the end of each month. Your "income" consists of all the money coming in regularly, while all the money going out represents your "expenses."

In March, as highlighted above, from your "side hustle," in this example, selling Lobsters (which Terry loves), you, however, earn a profit of $500, which means what is left from a business after all expenses have been paid. This means you should have extra money if you maintain the same level of expenditure. You can, therefore, save even more than usual and use this extra money for giving others (principle #4), making money work for you (principle #5), or for fun, for example, going on holiday (contentment, principle #6).

As you can see, because the rest of the principles heavily hinge upon budgeting, let this principle be the one you follow if you learn nothing else. I have seen from my experience with clients, including my millionaire and billionaire clients, and from my research that countless millions around the world start failing financially when they fail to start budgeting.

Money Principle #2: Spend less than you earn (saving and analysis)

This basic idea is often overlooked despite its apparent simplicity. Many of us are stuck in a vicious cycle of debt because our spending regularly exceeds our income, resulting in our borrowing. Still, you typically borrow with interest, which must be repaid to the lender, so now you have even less to spend on your own needs, so you are forced to borrow some more.

It doesn't help that in developed countries like the US; there is so much easy access to debt via credit cards, payday loans, and bank overdrafts, which, while serving a good purpose of rescuing many out of a difficult period, also keep many enslaved to the system.

By comparison, when you spend less than you earn, you save. And what you save becomes wealth. You must save money for a 'rainy day' – a rainy day being when the source of funds, for example, your job or 'the bank of mummy and daddy' suddenly disappears. Then, you can use your savings.

The budget tool in principle #1 will help you plan where your money should go. When you compare your budget to your actual expenditure, this is called "budget – actual variance analysis," You can start seeing where to make changes or how to start spending less than you earn if you haven't been aware of it. This concept of making a regular comparison of your budget is very critical!

I regularly review my bank statements as an example to help me monitor my spending patterns and see the "hidden problem areas" where actual expenditure may be higher than the budget but is not immediately apparent. For example, it's easy to overlook the cost of things like eating out or ordering takeout because they aren't as large or obvious as buying a car. If you, however, compare your actual spending to your budget regularly, you may be able to spot such hidden patterns.

Money Principle #3: Try not to borrow

Many of us today are not aware that following ancient principles, borrowing money is equivalent to being a slave to the lender, and boy, oh boy, is our country, the US, a nation of slaves. Please note, I am not talking about the ahem... King Kunta matter. Dave Ramsey, a well-known financial advisor, proposes seven baby steps to escape debt and become financially independent. They are:

- Save for a starter emergency fund (e.g., $1,000).
- Pay off all debt (except your mortgage).
- Save 3-6 months of expenses in a fully funded emergency fund.
- Invest 15% of your income into retirement.
- Save for your children's education (college fund).
- Pay off your mortgage early.
- Finally, build wealth and give.

Depth and dividends

If you have never saved money, you should start now. Don't put it off for another day. Get started saving for the unexpected, pay off debt as soon as possible, and build up your savings. These are the baby steps I should have taken earlier to avoid facing Mr. Azalia L.

Money principle #4: Give

Before someone is rich, they are poor, and someone helps them. For one person to become richer – someone somewhere else is often becoming poorer because resources that build wealth are often finite, that is, limited. So, when you are rich, you need to give to others – to help them, as I narrated with the example of Mr. Gates.

When you donate money, it flows like a river and eventually reaches the sea. The ocean's water evaporates into the air, condenses into clouds, and eventually falls to the earth as rain, replenishing the river's supply. I am deliberately using simplistic principles because sometimes that is the only way to reach the smartest ones – you, Mr./Mrs. Entrepreneur Extraordinaire.

Money principle #5: Let money work for you (investing)

Once you've covered your expenses and can account for any surplus cash you've made, as I demonstrated in the budget principle (#1), the fun begins! You can use the extra savings left to invest – or to "make the money work for you."

Making money work for you is simply this – whether you are sleeping or awake, you can make money. It is likely that most of the adults you know are unfortunately tied to daily jobs – where if they don't turn up, they don't earn. Likewise, where they own small, often family-run businesses, it is still the same – if they don't turn up at the business, they won't earn money.

Instead, the secret to many of the millionaires and billionaires I have seen and worked with is that they apply a different rule – the one where the money works for you. For example, Jeff Bezos has you buying items from *Amazon* day and night. He worked hard, yes, and still does, by setting up systems, but what he did was "automate the money-making." Automation of money-making means that the process is as automatic as possible, with limited human intervention.

The *Amazon* website, for example, uses a lot of Artificial Intelligence (AI). When you log on, it recognizes your username or allows biometric access. You don't need Mr. Bezos standing at a warehouse door to welcome you. When you start shopping, AI gives you "suggestions" based on your previous shopping experience; this is good customer care tailored to your needs. When you are shopping in your pajamas, Mr. Bezos is sleeping or wrestling with his own mortal enemies.

In fact, everything about the Amazon process has been automated as much as possible. From the ordering process to customer care, you often no longer chat with a human being but with an AI chatbot: "Hello, Maggie, what can I do for you?" There are even robots in their warehouses that automatically find the item you ordered and arrange for it to be packed and shipped to your address – using records automatically maintained on a computer, with no need for a trainee accountant to have to find your records and update your payment detail before the item ships.

Mr. Bezos is now sleeping, now dreaming, now waking and by this time he gets a notification that his wealth in Amazon shares has increased and he is making $x per second. There are 28,800 seconds in a standard 8-hour night of sleep recommended for an adult. His wealth by this time has increased by $x million while you were dreaming.

Entrepreneurship, with automated systems, is one of the ways you can really make money work for you, as I have explained above from Mr. Bezos' case. Still, additionally, there are many other things you can invest in that mimic the "make money work for you, principle," for example:

- You can keep it in a bank or a pension fund (for when you are in retirement). While there, it automatically generates a return for you (for example, interest).
- You can invest it in shares – other companies that use your money to make you more money and pay you 'dividends' – a reward when the business grows.
- You can invest it into trees. After the initial hard work, these mostly grow on their own – storing generational wealth for your grandchildren and protecting the environment in the process.

Please note, entrepreneur: Investments can go up or down. Past success does not equal future success.

Money Principle #6: Being content

The International Monetary Fund (IMF), for a fun task (ha!), asked people in certain countries around the world the centuries-old question, "Can money buy happiness?" Here are some responses:

Independent Financial Consultant - New Delhi, India

"Can money buy happiness? It certainly doesn't make one sad. If it comes my way, I'll be happy."

Retiree - London, United Kingdom

"Money cannot buy happiness. It doesn't solve your problems. It's all inside you, isn't it? I walk miles every day around London and it's all free, and I'm really happy doing that."

Self-employed - Abuja, Nigeria

"I think money can buy happiness, and here's why. Money, they say, is any item that is generally accepted for payment for goods and services. That means if you have to pay school fees, you need money. If you need a home for yourself, you need money. If you want to buy yourself something to eat, you need money. So, if you don't have money to get these things, there won't be happiness."

Doctor - Bogotá, Colombia

"Yes, money can buy happiness. There is a feeling in this country that if you have problems and at the same time you have some resources, it helps. Most of the problems of this country and the world are solved with money."

Retired Nurse - Moscow, Russia

"I think that money is evil. Money can't buy happiness. As long as there's happiness in the family, everyone gets along, relatives and close ones are healthy—for me, that's happiness."

When I was growing up, we struggled with the concept of income equality in the world, so my mother used a simple illustration. She held up her fingers and asked us: "Are these fingers equal?"

The lesson is that being happy with what you have is important because we are not equal. Do not be envious. Be happy, work hard, and do not worry if you are not the wealthiest person; remember: "The best things in life are free." Also – life is much more than money. Sometimes, you can work so hard to earn much money, and in the process – you forget your family; this is also not good, so find a balance (as Terry will tell you later).

I learned contentment from observing my mum at a time when we had no credit cards, no internet, no appeal to 'help a poor African mother,' no government social welfare program, no inheritance, and no lofty education accomplishments. All she had was a healthy attitude and a fire in her belly. Some might call her a silly and poor African woman. As for me, I think she just might be a black Bill Gates in the making. You just might be a bad Bill Gates in the making.

Money Principle #7: Identify recession-proof careers

Despite their best efforts, many people simply can't apply these money principles, let alone give money away if they don't have it in the first place!

As I narrated earlier, as an example, about 60% of Americans live from paycheck to paycheck.

One solution to this issue is identifying resilient careers during economic downturns that will likely remain in demand over the next two decades. This is especially critical in challenging economic times and technological advancements.

Below are ten such careers that are likely to remain in demand and thus continue to generate income. I also include the rationale for why they will continue to be in demand over the foreseeable future. Terry and I have been in resilient careers – he was in the military (public safety), and I was an accountant (financial services). We, therefore, understand what it means to be in the right career. You should, therefore, seek employment in **these ten sectors** to build up your skill set or consider setting up a business in similar sectors.

1. Healthcare Professionals

- Roles: Registered Nurses, Physicians, Medical Technicians
- Rationale: Healthcare services are indispensable, and an aging population will continue to drive demand.

2. Information Technology Specialists

- Roles: Cybersecurity Analysts, Software Developers, IT Support Specialists
- Rationale: As technology integrates further into daily life, the need for IT expertise grows.

3. Education Professionals

- Roles: Teachers, Educational Administrators, Curriculum Developers
- Rationale: Education remains a cornerstone of society, with ongoing demand for qualified educators.

4. Public Safety and Law Enforcement Officers

- Roles: Police Officers, Firefighters, Emergency Medical Technicians

- Rationale: Public safety is a constant priority, ensuring steady demand for these roles.

5. Utility Workers

- Roles: Electricians, Plumbers, Water Treatment Operators
- Rationale: Maintenance of essential services like electricity and water is critical, regardless of economic conditions.

6. Financial Services Professionals

- Roles: Accountants (CPAs), Auditors (Also CPAs), Financial Analysts.
- Rationale: Financial expertise is vital for both individuals and businesses to navigate economic challenges.

7. Mental Health Counselors

- Roles: Therapists, Psychologists, Social Workers
- Rationale: Increased awareness of mental health ensures ongoing need for these professionals.

8. Pharmaceutical and Biotechnology Researchers

- Roles: Pharmacists, Biochemists, Clinical Researchers
- Rationale: Continuous development of medical treatments and vaccines is essential for public health.

9. Environmental and Renewable Energy Specialists

- Roles: Environmental Engineers, Renewable Energy Technicians, Conservation Scientists
- Rationale: Growing focus on sustainability drives demand for expertise in these areas.

10. Supply Chain and Logistics Managers

- Roles: Logistics Coordinators, Supply Chain Analysts, Warehouse Managers
- Rationale: Efficient movement of goods is crucial, with e-commerce and global trade expansion sustaining these roles.

These careers not only offer resilience during economic downturns but are also poised to remain relevant as societal needs evolve over the next 20 years from the time of this book's writing.

In conclusion: applying the lessons

While written for an individual, the seven money principles can also be extrapolated to business. They also work irrespective of whether you are young or old, King Kunta or King Gates. Irrespective of your country or income level. They worked 2,000 years ago, work today, and will work tomorrow. Those principles, in summary, are:

- Money principle #1. Write things down (budgeting)
- Money principle #2. Spend less than you earn (saving and analysis)
- Money principle #3. Try not to borrow
- Money principle #4. Give
- Money principle #5. Let money work for you (investing)
- Money principle #6. Being content
- Money principle #7: Identify recession-proof careers

Cedric M, FCCA, erstwhile philosopher, was partially in the right but not wholly. If you sort your money out, you only partially sort out your life. You only tame the beast for a while. Instead of taking you to the celestial mountain, money makes you the king of discomfort. You then hear another unknown voice whisper: *"What use is it to gain the whole world and lose your soul?"* It was the season of slavery; it was the season of epiphanies. It was the best of times; it was the worst of times.

The universal principle above is supposed to make you realize that making money is not the end of it all; it is really part of something more, but that is not the subject of this book; maybe that will be the next business series book yours truly writes with Mr. Ingram!

Let me now hand you back to Terry, who will share the next step of his journey and how he navigated the transition from the seas to civilian life and employment. I will also leave you with a photo of my folks below, so see you later, landlubber (a person unfamiliar with the sea or sailing).

Wedding day of beloved Ol' daddy man Derek Wasake & my jack of all trades mother, Sarah (c. 1973)

Toolkit items you need at this stage (See Appendix I)

1. *Start-up budget template*
2. *Cash flow tracker*

CHAPTER 3
NAVIGATING THE SEAS OF CHANGE

Handling uncertainty

The journey from one career to another is akin to navigating uncharted waters. It's a voyage filled with uncertainty, challenges, and opportunities for growth. For those leaving military service, for example, and entering the civilian workforce, this transition can be particularly daunting. The structured environment of the military, with its clear chain of command and well-defined roles, often contrasts sharply with the more fluid and sometimes ambiguous nature of civilian workplaces.

My journey from the US submarine service to the civilian world serves as a testament to both the challenges and the immense growth potential that such transitions offer. When I first left the military, I was convinced that my extensive training and education had prepared me for anything the civilian world could throw at me, like those who graduated with degrees. After all, I had received some of the best training in process control equipment, mechanical engineering, and electrical engineering—comparable to or even surpassing what most would acquire with a master's degree through traditional academia.

This confidence, while not entirely misplaced, would soon be tested in ways I couldn't have anticipated. In retrospect, my initial overconfidence was a classic example of the Dunning-Kruger effect—a cognitive bias where individuals with limited knowledge or expertise in a specific domain overestimate their abilities. This phenomenon is particularly common in career transitions, where individuals may not fully grasp the nuances and complexities of their new field or role, such as an entrepreneur.

For those transitioning from the military to civilian roles, this effect can be even more pronounced. The highly specialized skills and knowledge acquired in military service are invaluable, but they don't always translate directly to civilian contexts. Understanding this cognitive bias can help transitioning professionals approach their new roles with a more balanced perspective, combining confidence in their abilities with an openness to learning and adaptation. This, too, does not exempt the transitions to other careers but solidifies the proper understanding of what reality is – as my moment of truth story below shows.

My experience: "No means I'll see you next Tuesday."

My moment of truth came just 30 days after departing the military. I had secured a job as a sales engineer, calling on multiple industries from pulp and paper to power, pharmaceutical, food and beverage, and chemical. Convinced of my abilities, I spent three weeks in product training; I set out to attend a sales meeting solo with a leading manufacturer in the cosmetics industry specializing in hair replacement products.

With all the vigor I had in me, studying the processes from what I could find and read, I was determined to make all my experiences culminate into success. I remember telling my wife, "This is a huge opportunity to secure a large order." I headed out on my mission, steadfast in what I was confident that I knew.

When arriving at the facility, I had this glow of confidence. I worked my way through security and throughout the plant, walking, looking, and observing in awe of all the processes, confident that I understood enough that I would not be questioned but heard loud and clear. After all, I had spent a great deal of my time learning, living, and working in process spaces.

Chapter 3: Navigating the Seas of Change

After a short walk, I ended up in an office with the head of procurement on the backside of a massive warehouse. I waited diligently and again with confidence for the procurement manager to arrive. This was the day that reality hit: I didn't know what I didn't know.

I had the opportunity to talk about some specialty products for very corrosive applications. I felt confident in my delivery and my answers. But as the meeting progressed, I found myself being drilled like I was sitting for my board to get my insignia dolphins years prior. This procurement manager understood this plant probably better than most inside the plant itself. He asked me such difficult questions, and I had nowhere to go. His blood was boiling; I was wasting his time. And I found myself totally destroyed internally.

I'd let myself down, the business down, and most importantly, my family. After he raised his voice multiple times, explaining how my incompetence was not accepted and questioning why somebody would send me out without the necessary knowledge to articulate some of the critical values of the products, I was reeling. Of course, this gentleman knew more than anybody about the key factors that made these products unique because he had been buying them for 25 years. He knew every question to ask, every difficult answer that needed to follow, and threw them at me one after another.

At the end of our meeting, he asked me not to come back to avoid any more confusion. As I sat there calmly and in total embarrassment, he ended the meeting abruptly. I stood up and told him that I would see him next Tuesday with every single answer to the questions he had asked me. I would be more prepared. He refused immediately, making it very clear that I was not welcome back.

This experience was a pivotal moment in my transition from military to civilian life. It taught me several valuable lessons that would shape my future career. First and foremost, it highlighted the danger of overconfidence. While

Depth and dividends

the military had trained me to project confidence and decisiveness, I learned that in the civilian business world, admitting to not knowing something could be a strength rather than a weakness.

Secondly, it underscored the value of industry-specific knowledge. While my technical background was strong, I lacked the specific industry knowledge that was crucial for success in this role. This highlighted the importance of continuous learning and preparation. In any new field, there's a wealth of industry-specific knowledge that can only be acquired through experience and dedicated study, and let's be clear: this never ends, even for the entrepreneur.

Chapter 3: Navigating the Seas of Change

The procurement manager's deep knowledge, built over decades in the industry, showed me the irreplaceable value of experience. It was a stark reminder that no amount of general education can fully prepare you for the nuances of a specific field. This realization helped me develop a deep respect for industry veterans and a hunger to accumulate my own experiential knowledge.

This experience was the beginning of a new chapter in my career. It was the moment I realized that what I thought I knew, I really did not. But more importantly, it instilled in me a motto that I carried for the rest of my career: "No means I'll see you next Tuesday." I have found myself telling this story at every level in companies, instilling in them that it's okay not to know everything but that it is your responsibility to surround yourself with more intelligent people than you and then learn and share.

I went home demoralized and frustrated. I told my wife that I was going to quit my job; I was not ready. She asked me to call the office and speak to my mentor and my boss at the time. This happened on a Tuesday, and I was determined to move on and look for another job. But instead, my boss told me to stay home, continue reading, and sent me information. We met over the weekend to prepare.

I explained to him that there was no way I was going to get back in, but I did tell him that I had told the purchasing director that I was coming back. He encouraged me to do my best to get back in the building to show him that although I didn't have the answers, I knew where to get them.

Despite the humiliating experience, I didn't give up. My instinct to offer to return with better answers, even when rebuffed, demonstrated the resilience that would be crucial in navigating my career. This resilience, ingrained through military training, proved to be one of the most valuable assets in my civilian career. Lastly, this experience underscored the need not just to possess knowledge but to effectively communicate it in a way that resonates with the audience. It's not just about what you know but how you convey it. In the military, communication often follows strict protocols. In the civilian world, I had to learn to adapt my communication style to various audiences and contexts.

The following Tuesday, I arose with all the vigor I had the previous Tuesday and went to the plant again. Security wouldn't let me in the plant because I was on the no-entry list. However, after discussing with the security guards, they saw that I needed to finish what I started and allowed me to pass through at the risk of being reprimanded for letting me in; they knew the purchasing director well, so they afforded me one last shot.

I arrived at the warehouse and walked straight into the back of the building. While I was there, I realized I was going into the hornet's nest. I arrived, walked in, and there was a couch to my left. I sat down and looked straight at a desk where nobody was sitting. I waited about 35 to 40 minutes. I remember this time because it was the longest time I could ever imagine in my career that I had to do something and wait for the principal, as some might think, to come back to meet me.

He walked into this office, didn't notice me, sat down, looked straight across his desk, and saw me. His voice raised. He was just sheer livid that I got in the plant and that I was willing to sit there and not get up and walk out. I asked him repeatedly to please let me answer the questions that I told him last week I would get for him. After that, I said to him that I would be happy to leave and not return.

He bantered with me for a good 15 minutes in a very aggressive but professional way and then yielded and allowed me to go through the questions he had asked me one by one. I went through them with as much specificity as I could. He looked at me intensely with a huge frown on his face. Once I was finished, I stood up and thanked him for the opportunity to clarify my ignorance and understanding that I didn't know what I didn't know, but today I did.

He then turned a smile on his face, looked at me, and asked me to sit back down. Then, he began to laugh and talk about my tenacity and my commitment to learning and not being embarrassed. He told me he had not cut the purchase order, which was for almost $100,000, to a competitor because he had been busy. He looked at me with great intensity and told me that he was going to award me the contract. In return, I needed to spend more time at the plant working with the operators to learn about his facility so that in the future, I would have more awareness.

The importance of mentors

One of the most crucial factors in my successful transition was the guidance and support of mentors. My boss's response to my initial failure was not to berate me or suggest I wasn't cut out for the job. Instead, he provided actionable steps to improve and encouraged me to try again. This experience highlighted the importance of effective mentorship in career transitions.

A good mentor provides honest, constructive feedback. They don't shy away from pointing out areas for improvement, but they do so in a way that motivates rather than discourages. Influential mentors don't just identify problems; they help develop solutions. My boss didn't just tell me I needed to improve; he provided resources and a plan for how to do so.

Mentors play a crucial role in boosting confidence and providing emotional support during challenging times. My boss's belief in my ability to turn the situation around was a powerful motivator. Through his handling of the situation, he demonstrated the kind of leadership I would strive to embody later in my career. He showed me that good leaders support their team members through failures and help them learn from these experiences.

Perhaps most importantly, my mentor saw this failure not as a terminal event but as a learning opportunity that could contribute to long-term growth. This long-term perspective is crucial for effective mentorship and leadership.

My experience transitioning from military to civilian life taught me that learning is a lifelong process. This realization became a driving force in my career development. Rather than fearing or hiding what you don't know, I learned to view it as an opportunity to grow. Admitting ignorance opens the door to new knowledge and experiences.

I also learned not to limit myself to formal education or training. Some of the most valuable learning comes from on-the-job experiences, conversations with colleagues, and even failures. Taking time to reflect on experiences, both successes and failures, became a crucial part of my learning process, as it still is today. I would ask myself what I've learned and how I can apply these lessons in the future.

Cultivating a sense of curiosity about my industry, my role, and the world at large became a habit. Curious people are lifelong learners who continually expand their knowledge and skills. I also discovered that teaching others is one of the best ways to reinforce your own learning. I began to look for opportunities to share my knowledge and experiences with colleagues or mentees.

Just a few years after this pivotal experience, I was promoted to vice president of sales. During the conversation about my promotion, it was brought to my attention that my transformation from a young sailor to a young executive was attributed to several key factors: my eagerness to learn, my willingness to lead, and, most importantly, my humbleness.

About humility

Throughout my career journey, I've come to recognize humility as a crucial leadership trait. Initially, I saw my moments of humility—admitting ignorance and facing failure—as weaknesses. However, I came to understand that these were actually strengths that contributed significantly to my growth as a leader.

Humble leaders remain open to learning from others, regardless of their position or experience level. This openness fosters an environment of continuous improvement and innovation. When leaders admit their mistakes or limitations, it builds trust with their team. It shows that it's okay to be imperfect and encourages honest communication.

Humble leaders are more likely to empower their team members, recognizing and valuing the strengths and contributions of others. A humble approach allows leaders to adapt more quickly to changing circumstances, as they're not bound by the need to always appear infallible. Humility is also closely linked to emotional intelligence. Humble leaders tend to be more self-aware and better at managing relationships.

The journey from a newly discharged sailor to a vice president of sales was not a straight line. It was a path marked by challenges, failures, and continuous learning. Each experience, whether a success or a setback, contributed to my transformation and growth.

The most valuable lesson I learned was that transformation is not a destination but a continuous journey. It's about constantly evolving, learning from every experience, and never assuming that one has all the answers. This mindset, cultivated through the crucible of early career challenges, became the cornerstone of my approach to leadership and continued professional growth.

As we move forward in this book, we'll explore more aspects of how transformation builds careers, delving into leadership, decision-making, and the ongoing process of personal and professional development. Each chapter will offer new insights and strategies for navigating the complex, ever-changing landscape of modern careers, always with an eye toward continuous growth and transformation.

Remember, your career journey is unique to you. The experiences and lessons shared in this chapter are meant to inspire and guide, but your path will have its twists and turns. Embrace them, learn from them, and let them fuel your transformation. The sea of career change may be challenging to navigate, but with persistence, humility, and a commitment to continuous learning, you can chart a course to success.

Lesson conclusion: How Will You Navigate Your Professional Seas?

As we reflect on the journey from a newly discharged sailor to a vice president of sales, it's clear that transformation in our careers is not just about acquiring new skills but about fundamentally changing our approach to challenges and learning. Consider the pivotal moment in that cosmetics manufacturing plant - a humbling experience that could have derailed a career but instead became a catalyst for growth.

In this area, you can learn from after-action reviews (AARs). The Navy conducts AARs to assess operations and identify improvements. Implementing AARs in business encourages continuous learning and process enhancement – as my experience showed, I went back home to learn and continuously improve, but as part of that, I got to know the industry as much as possible, so this is where you need two tool kits (See *Appendix I*) – a compliance checklist so you know the industry and a crisis response plan so that you can handle, well crises.

How might you turn your professional setbacks into opportunities for learning and advancement for your team? The persistence to return to that plant, despite explicit rejection, exemplifies the kind of tenacity that can define a career. In your own professional life, where might you apply this "No means I'll see you next Tuesday" attitude?

You could also, if you want, employ the military's Rules of Engagement (ROE). The Navy establishes ROE to guide interactions. Setting clear guidelines and understanding acceptable terms in business negotiations can lead to successful deals, including setting ROE for difficult situations, negotiations, and deals.

I also mentioned that the role of mentorship was crucial in this journey. Reflect on the guidance provided by the boss who, instead of criticism, offered support and a path forward. This type of mentorship goes beyond mere advice; it's about delivering actionable steps and believing in potential. As you progress in your career, consider how to seek out such mentorship and how you might provide it to others. Are you surrounding yourself with mentors who challenge you to grow? Are you, in turn, fostering the growth of those around you? Are you making this a priority every day?

For entrepreneurs, this lesson underscores a critical truth: no one succeeds alone. The complexities of building and leading a business demand more than just individual effort and knowledge. They require a network of mentors and advisors who can provide diverse perspectives, challenge your thinking, and offer guidance based on their own experiences. As a business leader, how are you actively seeking out and engaging with mentors and advisors?

These external voices are not just sounding boards; they are catalysts for growth, offering insights that can help you navigate challenges more effectively and identify opportunities you might otherwise miss. Let them in the door, actively participate in change, and you will see new insights that will amaze you.

Moreover, by embracing mentorship and external advice, you're not just developing yourself but also being a role model and establishing a growth mindset for your entire organization. This approach can create a ripple effect, fostering a culture of continuous learning and improvement throughout your team. Consider how bringing in advisors or delegating specific responsibilities could free you to focus on strategic growth. Are you leveraging these resources to their fullest potential?

Remember, the most successful entrepreneurs are often those who recognize the limitations of their time and knowledge and actively seek to expand their understanding and capabilities through the wisdom of others.

Depth and dividends

One navy strategy you can employ in business is Resource Allocation and Prioritization. The Navy meticulously allocates resources to ensure mission success. Similarly, in business, you should prioritize financial resources to areas that yield the highest return on investment.

Otherwise, the transition from military to civilian life highlighted the importance of continuous learning and adaptability. The realization that extensive military training didn't directly translate to civilian industry knowledge was a turning point. In your career, how are you addressing gaps in your knowledge? Are you actively seeking out industry-specific information and experiences?

Remember, admitting what you don't know is often the first step toward acquiring valuable new skills and insights.

For entrepreneurs and business leaders, this story offers particularly poignant lessons. The initial overconfidence followed by a harsh reality check mirrors the experiences many face when starting or growing a business. How often do you step out of your comfort zone to gain new perspectives on your business? Are you, like the procurement manager, deeply knowledgeable about every aspect of your operation, or are there areas where you need to deepen your understanding? That latter is more often than not.

Humility emerged as a critical leadership trait through these experiences. The willingness to admit ignorance, to learn from every interaction, and to persist in the face of failure all stem from a humble approach to career growth. As you lead your team or run your business, how can you cultivate this type of humility? How might it change your approach to decision-making, team-building, or problem-solving?

Ultimately, the transformation described in this chapter wasn't just about moving from one role to another but about developing a mindset of continuous growth and adaptability. As you progress in your career, consider how to embed these principles into your daily practice. How can you ensure that each experience, whether a success or a setback, contributes to your ongoing transformation? By surrounding yourself with the right mentors and advisors, you're not just solving immediate problems – you're building a foundation for long-term success and resilience in the face of an ever-changing business landscape.

By constantly evolving, learning from every experience, and never assuming you have all the answers, you, too, can navigate the complex seas of industry change and chart a course to success. The question remains: how will you leverage the power of mentorship, continuous learning, and humility to transform your career and business?

Toolkit items you need at this stage (See Appendix I)

1. *Compliance checklist*
2. *Crisis response framework*

CHAPTER 4
SECRETS MILLIONAIRES USE TO SELL MORE

Shall we do an After-Action Review (AAR) for Terry's "See You Next Tuesday" moment?

When we concluded the last chapter of Terry's story, he offered you a critical way to overcome challenges. He mentioned that you can learn from the military's **After-Action Reviews (AAR),** where the Navy conducts AARs to assess operations and identify improvements.

In that chapter, he shared a seminal moment of how he was humiliated when he tried to sell to an angry potential customer with overconfidence or cognitive bias, and he eventually said, "See you next Tuesday." In that story, there are some **critical highlights** I want to dissect and analyze with you:

> *After he raised his voice multiple times, explaining how my incompetence was not accepted and questioning why somebody would send me out without the necessary knowledge to articulate some of the critical values of the products, I was reeling.*
>
> *....it underscored the value of industry-specific knowledge. While my technical background was strong, I lacked the specific industry knowledge that was crucial for success in this role. This highlighted the importance of continuous learning and preparation.*

Depth and dividends

> ....*Lastly, this experience underscored the need not just to possess knowledge but to effectively communicate it in a way that resonates with the audience. It's not just about what you know but how you convey it.*

Terry is ultimately speaking about how you communicate or, more importantly, how you sell/market a product or service. It is not just the knowledge you must acquire and convey – you must learn what works well and what does not.

Marketing/selling insights from an accountant?

You are probably wondering why, as an accountant, I am not telling you the "boring stuff" of double entry and how to cut costs. Instead, I am spending much time on selling/marketing, which should have been Terry's turf.

Well, you see, the fact is this: the numbers in business do not lie. Businesses fail (and I will come to that in another chapter) because they do not sell enough to cover their expenses.

I have seen it happen in plenty of businesses. The idea is brilliant, but there are just not enough sales, so management keeps cutting costs until they go out of business.

Many accountants focus on the cost-cutting stuff (which is important too), but what use is it to cut costs if you need more revenue in the first place to sustain your business? And the reality is this: If you are in business (rather than an NGO or charity), you have one primary aim: to sell more.

Sure, sustainability is critical, but selling more to make a profit is the lifeblood of business. It is not very wise to borrow, as I narrated earlier, and as such, selling more seems like the only critical means of growing your business. It is why I am passionate about sales. Much of the information I am about to provide comes from two of the world's leading marketing experts (BUT backed up by my experience).

This stuff works

I am not providing it because it is from some "best-selling" book or so-called "marketing guru," but mainly because, plain and simple, this stuff works. It worked for previous employers I worked with when we tested it, and it works for Terry and me.

It can work for your business or organization as well. Hopefully, instead of ignoring this, you will choose the "lazy" option to try these principles and save yourself loads of years of wasted effort of trial and error.

About these "sales" men.

Depth and dividends

Andy Bounds is half-blind. His other "good eye" has limited vision, so he cannot, for example, drive himself. His blindness is hereditary. He, however, won Britain's "Sales Trainer of the Year." He explains that he is good because he had to explain things to his blind mother. He, therefore, sees things differently (no pun intended).

I have met Andy (twice) and bought his best-seller book, The Jelly Effect. I read his stuff because it works—it is simple yet powerful. Last I checked, Andy typically charges £5,000 an hour for consultation. Yes, you read right—£5,000 per hour!

The second is Chris Cardell. Chris has spent at least $1 million on Google advertising and is considered one of the world's leading marketers. He helps his clients (many of whom are millionaires) achieve up to 200% profits. I was once a member of Chris's Inner VIP members' club. I read (and watch) his stuff because it works - it is simple yet powerful.

What are some of Andy's tips for selling more?
1. The AFTERs-based principle.

"Clients want problem solvers, not technicians," or put rather more bluntly: "Customers don't care what you do. They care about what they're left with AFTER you have done it."

Why is this stuff powerful?

When you focus on what a customer is receiving, i.e., the BENEFITS of your product/services (saving time, saving money, less stress), you will stop focusing on stuff they don't really care about, i.e., the features of your product (we are the best, the smartest, the fastest, the largest, etc.). Terry leveraged this the second time around to get the buyer's attention. He learned all he could so he could articulate benefits.

When you focus on what your customers want, you instantly become more interesting to them, and they are more likely to come to you because you are solving their problems. They don't really care if, for example, you are the best submariner in the world (though that helps); they really care that you can solve the problem efficiently.

Action point: Think of your customers. What do they really want? What are the benefits of your product or service? After identifying this clearly (think, for example, of 4-7 benefits), work backward to determine how your product/service meets their needs (i.e., benefits them).

2. How do you use your AFTERS to sell more?

There are two things your customers want when making a buying decision.

1. Their desired AFTERs and;
2. Absolute certainty that you can provide their AFTERS.

These are the only two things customers are interested in.

If they know with 100% certainty that they will get the AFTERS they require, they will buy.

This means traditional selling approaches like "we were formed in 1993" or "we are the best manufacturer of x" do not satisfy this criterion and do NOTHING to provide certainty that you can deliver a customer's AFTERS.

To sell, therefore, you need to remember the **ABC** principle:

- **A**fters: Establish the customers' AFTERS. Ask the customer what they want, for example, "What are you looking to achieve AFTER working with us?" "How would you judge this project a success?"
- **B**e Certain. State with certainty that you can provide these AFTERS (this is a simple stage), but first clarify that you understand and then say it, for example: "Well, I can definitely help you."
- **C**onvince. Prove that you can deliver those AFTERS. This is where you have a bank of proof, e.g., testimonials and client case studies, but this time, you have restructured them to show how they meet the customer's benefits.

Depth and dividends

You might already have much of the information (experience, case studies, etc.). What you need to do, however, is restructure it to first focus on what the client wants and then show how exactly you meet their AFTERS (needs).

Action point: Review your sales material or the next proposal you submit with the AFTERS hat on. Does it meet the above test? If not, you need to restructure it from the customer's perspective.

What are some of Chris's tips for selling more?

1. Make your customers loyal.

Try these two principles:

a. Mail them frequent, interesting, and informative information (not necessarily selling to them). You can do this via a newsletter.

b. Position yourself as an authority. For example, have a regular column in the newspaper.

2. Get your competitors to introduce you to their customers.

It sounds crazy, but hopefully, you have a prospect list (potential clients). Despite your best efforts, you conclude that no matter what you do, some people are just not going to buy from you. These are the "nonbuyers." You have spent a lot of money on them (and time), but they are worth nothing to you. Here is where you can be clever: Offer to trade your nonbuyers to your competitors in return for their nonbuyer's list. Yes, it sounds crazy, but these non-buyers mean nothing to you, so by swapping, you stand some chance of getting trade value from them.

3. Give to receive.

Instead of running your ads and other pieces with the intention of making an immediate sale, give something FREE (a free report, a sample with no obligation) to BEGIN A RELATIONSHIP.

4. Sell effectively and with integrity.

A sale is about service, not just selling. "You will get what you want in life if you help other people get what they want."

5. Don't give up too soon.

Some statistics to scare you.

- 48% of salespeople never follow up with a prospect
- 25% of salespeople make a second contact and stop
- 12% of salespeople only make three contacts and stop.

Only 10% of businesses make more than three contacts. This means you are losing a small fortune because:

- 2% of sales are made on the first contact
- 3% of sales are made on the second contact
- 5% of sales are made on the third contact
- 10% of sales are made on the fourth contact
- 80% of sales are made on the fifth to twelfth contact

Terry spoke of this – he did not give up too soon, neither should you.

6. Use your time wisely.

Not every prospect is equal. It sounds unfair or wrong, but it's true. The 80/20 rule is that 80 % of your business will come from 20% of your customers. It is a fact that some people will give you $100m, and others will never amount to much. Focus your attention on finding those potentials (the 20%) who will be the "best customers." Those who will repeatedly give you a lot of money with minimum effort.

Depth and dividends

Terry implemented this strategy as well. This client gave him an order so big that it made the effort worthwhile!

Special section: The rise of digital marketing and permission-based marketing

The continued rise of the internet and the increased use of mobile phones mean that customers are increasingly being bombarded with marketing information. This means that the immediate sale rarely works. Lead generation is, therefore, the way to go. What is Lead Generation?

In principle, the customer comes to you, and they need more information. You provide it and then ask them (for permission) to start a relationship with you. How do you give this information? How about using SMS-based permission marketing? Why? "SMS has an almost 100% read rate; you read virtually every SMS you get".

How about e-mail? Bulk E-mail marketing programs like *Klaviyo* and *MailChimp* allow users to send bulk e-mail cheaply. Watch out, though! Research shows that 77% of marketers prefer email marketing, but according to their other research on email, the average user receives 78 emails a day! In an 8-hour working day, this is about ten emails an hour. This means that the most essential thing is the subject line. No matter how well-written the body of your email is, the recipient must perceive an immediate benefit if you expect them even to open it.

For every SMS or email marketing (or other email you send), make sure the subject line (or first few lines) makes the recipient want to open it or ask for more information.

Digital marketing, and notably content marketing as a strategy, uses the permission-based model. This means that if you give high-quality content, the person will ask for more information and thus give you permission to market to them.

Many successful businesses increasingly use this model for selling because Most Small and Medium Enterprises (SMEs) do not have the advertising budget of, say, Coca-Cola to invest in TV, Times Square Billboards, Newspapers, etc., but they can invest in Digital Marketing strategies such as e-mail marketing, which is much cheaper than the traditional approaches, and so you get a bigger return on investment.

So, what are the Digital Marketing Strategies?

They include some of the following:

1. *Content Marketing or Thought Leadership* - Blogs, whitepapers, and infographics that build trust.

2. *SEO (Search Engine Optimization)* - Drives visibility on search engines using keywords.

3. *Search Engine Marketing (SEM) & PPC (Pay-Per-Click)* - Targets high-intent clients with ads, e.g., Google Ads, Facebook, *or LinkedIn Ads.*

4. *Social Media Marketing-* Engages audiences on *LinkedIn, Facebook, YouTube, TikTok, Instagram, etc.*

5. *Email Marketing* Nurtures relationships through newsletters and campaigns. If possible, emails are automated using providers such as *Klaviyo and Mailchimp.*

6. *Video Marketing* - Webinars, explainer videos, and live sessions to demonstrate expertise.

7. *Webinars & Online Events* - Real-time sessions with prospective clients.

8. *Influencer Marketing* - Leverages industry leaders to boost credibility.

9. *Retargeting Ads*—Re-engage visitors who have shown interest, especially on SEM and PPC (see three above).

10. *Podcasting* - Builds loyalty through regular insights and industry discussions.

11. *Lead Generation Forms & Chatbots* - Captures information and engages website visitors.

12. *Public Relations & Online Reputation Management* - Builds credibility and manages reviews.

13. *Conversion Rate Optimization (CRO)* - Improves lead generation on landing pages.

14. *Affiliate Marketing* - Drives traffic through referrals.

15. *Community Building* - Engages audiences on social platforms and forums.

16. *Data Analytics & Insights* - Tracks and optimizes strategy performance.

Does Digital Marketing work?

I am absolutely sure that it works because I have implemented many of the strategies I have highlighted and seen tremendous growth for the organizations I worked for.

In addition, below, I provide example case studies of reputable brands and companies you likely know and the specific digital strategies they have used to prove that these millionaire companies are using the same strategies. You will be surprised that now that you know the strategies by type, your eyes will be opened to see that all major brands indeed use them. So here is the secret - the millionaires are using these same strategies to sell more, just that they have bigger budgets. So, get smart and copy the strategies! Here are some of the successful brands you can copy from and the strategies they follow:

Consulting: McKinsey & Company

- Strategy: In-depth articles and email newsletters.
- Outcome: 25% increase in traffic and a 12% rise in inquiries.

Information Technology: IBM

- Strategy: SEO, SEM, webinars, and video marketing.
- Outcome: 30% lead growth and 15% boost in conversion rates.

Healthcare: Mayo Clinic

- Strategy: Content marketing with health blogs and videos.
- Outcome: 35% increase in site traffic and 20% rise in patient inquiries.

Real Estate: Zillow

- Strategy: SEO and content.
- Outcome: 50% traffic increase and 30% rise in engagement.

Science & Research: National Geographic Society

- Strategy: Content marketing through articles and documentaries, shared across website and social channels.
- Outcome: 35% growth in website traffic and a 20% increase in subscriber engagement, driven by visually rich, informative content.

Economics & Policy: Brookings Institution

- Strategy: Published research and policy insights through content marketing, SEO, and social media.
- Outcome: 25% growth in online readership and a 30% increase in social media followers, expanding policy influence.

Lesson conclusion

Try to implement at least one of the weekly strategies and see how it works. Then move on to the next. Within no time, you will have sales growing by over 100%. Doing market research, including the tool in Appendix I, can help you build the order in which you implement the strategies or tailor them for your target customer. Also, the Risk Assessment tool will help you refine your marketing strategies by understanding the market risks.

See – an accountant can indeed give marketing tips! Of course, helped by marketing pros, but to be honest, I have done courses on digital marketing.

And now I will hand you back to Terry. He will describe how he moved to another level and the challenges he faced even there. Oh boy, the After-Action Review (AAR) will need to continue. See you next Tuesday!

Toolkit items you need at this stage (See Appendix I)

1. *Market research template*
2. *Risk Assessment template*

CHAPTER 5
ARE YOU READY TO TAKE THE HELM?

The call to leadership

The call to leadership, whether as a CEO, entrepreneur, steering a startup, or as a team leader within an established organization, is a siren song that many hear but few genuinely answer. My path into leadership serves as a stark reminder of this truth, illustrating the complexities and challenges that come with taking the helm.

Being a leader is far more complex than simply being a boss, as I mentioned above. It's one of the most intricate roles within any organization, laden with a multitude of responsibilities, conflicting characters, emotional unknowns, and countless other challenges. It's a balancing act that requires both strength and sensitivity, vision, and attention to detail.

As an example, There's a significant difference between the world of outside sales and the world of inside sales and operations, a distinction I hadn't fully grasped early on in my career.

These differences extend to how each role is perceived by upper management and how they're managed day-to-day. While outside sales focuses on building relationships, creating solutions in the field, securing profitable orders, and representing the company to clients, inside sales is the engine that keeps the business running smoothly.

Depth and dividends

Inside sales teams are focused on execution, fulfilling the promises made by their outside counterparts. They're constantly inundated with a multitude of tasks: preparing proposals, processing orders, ensuring equipment flow, coordinating technicians on site, and handling a plethora of challenges when customers aren't satisfied. They're in the line of fire. Yes, I said it; it is not outside sales; inside deals with the nitty-gritty details that can make or break a company's reputation.

In each quadrant of a business, some dynamics drive people's motivation to work hard and stay engaged, and some factors push them away. As a leader, it's your responsibility to understand these dynamics and use them to create an environment where your team can thrive.

My humble pie experience

Early in my career, I was offered an opportunity that seemed to embody all the challenges of leadership. I was invited to apply at a leading industrial distribution company in New England as the inside sales leader for a very seasoned team in a significant market. It was a step up even from my previous role of VP of Sales (outside sales) because it also required operational prowess and direction.

The role seemed tailor-made for my ambitions: they needed someone to drive organizational skills, foster better communication, and motivate long-time employees while bringing up the next generation.

Before I delve further into this experience, I want to emphasize why I'm sharing this part of my career path that very few know even today. My intent in humbly expressing these challenges is to assure others that they are not alone in facing difficult moments in their leadership journey.

Many might find it very difficult to have these conversations that are, at times, genuinely demoralizing or, more accurately, challenging to one's ego and those looking to them for leadership. However, I firmly believe that these experiences should not be seen as flaws in one's career but as opportunities for growth and professional development. By sharing my story, I hope to encourage others to embrace their challenges, learn from them, share them, and recognize them as crucial steps in their leadership evolution.

Prior to taking on this role, I had accumulated years of experience equally both in and out of the military. I had worked closely with outside the factory principals that we represented, salespeople, making sales calls to customers, driving business solutions, and, from my perspective, motivating a team. I thought I was ready. However, I was about to learn a crucial lesson about the nuances of different leadership roles within an organization.

Freshly out four years or so from my military experience and confident in my abilities, I felt more than ready to take on this challenge. After an extensive interview process and technical knowledge, including a Myers-Briggs assessment tool, I competed against both internal candidates from other divisions and external applicants. To my delight, I landed the position. Eager to embark on this new chapter, I informed my current boss of my decision to move on. His response was not what I expected.

With grace and concern, he sat me down and told me that I wasn't ready. He believed I needed more time to develop my leadership skills. It wasn't that I was a poor leader, he explained, but the role I was stepping into involved managing people who had been in the industry for years. They would, in his words, "run circles around me." He feared I lacked the necessary skill set to be successful.

But, true to my nature and the "No is not in my vocabulary" attitude I'd cultivated, I decided to forge ahead. I left the company and began my new role weeks later. This decision would soon teach me a valuable lesson about the pitfalls that await new leaders. No mentor in the wings and flying solo because they expected me to lead after all.

Initially, everything seemed perfect. My new colleagues were warm and accommodating, eager to get to work. But over time, I began to realize there was a game afoot. It wasn't malicious but rather a form of self-preservation.

Depth and dividends

They knew what I didn't know, and this knowledge gap became increasingly apparent.

As the weeks passed, my frustrations grew. I held countless meetings, trying to establish my authority and implement changes. However, I lacked a crucial understanding: the civilian workforce operates differently from the military. In the service, when you ask someone to do something, you expect it to be done promptly and without question. In the corporate world, things work differently. This is not to say that you needed to be in the military to be hard, direct, or frankly demanding; it's universal when you do not know how to lead.

Many new leaders, driven by the pressure to succeed and prove themselves, fall into the trap of unnecessary aggression or inflexibility. This often stems from a lack of experience or a misguided attempt to assert authority. In my case, I struggled to adapt my leadership style to a team that was much smarter than me.

Chapter 5: Are You Ready To Take The Helm?

Again, another significant point is to always surround yourself with people who are more intelligent than you and listen, but failing to recognize that what worked in the military and outside sales might not be effective in a corporate office setting.

After about six weeks of grinding hard and trying to build relationships, working insane hours, I was called into the owner's office. Sitting with him and his assistant of nearly 40 years, they delivered the news: I wasn't ready. They believed I had the mental and technical aptitude but lacked the necessary skill set to lead effectively in their organization. Had I heard this from someone else before?

I was perplexed. During my years in the military, instilled in me there was a strong understanding of roles, responsibilities, and accountability. However, as they pointed out, the real world operates by different rules. The owner, a kind gentleman, informed me that he had already spoken to my previous employer, who was eager to have me back. He asked me to prepare for an exit by the end of the week. At the same time, he told me to keep my head high and my future bright.

This was a tremendous blow. I was floored, not so much by the decision itself but by my failure to see my unreadiness. A week later, I found myself back in my old life, on the road, eager to see my customers and do what I did best at the time: produce solutions to challenging problems. The owner greeted me with a smile, handed me my car keys (my belongings were still in my car and inside the plant, almost like he knew I would be back), and told me to get back to work. "The time wasn't right," he said, "but I'm proud of you for giving it a try. Now, focus on what you've learned."

This experience taught me a crucial lesson about leadership: readiness isn't just about technical skills or even past leadership experience. It's about understanding the specific context of your leadership role, the people you're leading, and the organizational culture you're operating within.

While I was confident in my knowledge of the industries we served, I lacked a deep understanding of the dynamics of an inside sales role. As I mentioned, it had nothing to do with my technical aptitude or my ability to lead in general. It was my lack of understanding of what was necessary to lead in that specific context.

Leadership challenges at different levels

The call to leadership in my heartfelt, challenging words echoes through every level of an organization, from the CEO's office to the frontline supervisor's station. It's a summons that resonates with seasoned executives steering multinational corporations, entrepreneurs launching bold startups, middle managers orchestrating departmental success, and team leaders guiding small groups toward daily goals. Each leadership role, regardless of its place in the organizational hierarchy, carries its own set of challenges, responsibilities, and opportunities for impact.

At the apex, CEOs grapple with setting overarching visions, making high-stakes decisions that can alter the course of entire industries, and bearing the ultimate responsibility for their organization's success or failure. They must navigate complex market dynamics, stakeholder expectations, and the weighty task of shaping organizational culture from the top down.

Entrepreneurs, whether helming fledgling startups or guiding established businesses through periods of growth and change, face the unique pressures of wearing multiple hats. They must be visionaries, strategists, salespeople, and sometimes even janitors, all while building a team and a culture from the ground up.

In the middle tiers of leadership, executives and managers serve as crucial links between upper management's strategic directives and the day-to-day operations that bring those strategies to life. They translate broad organizational goals into actionable plans, balance the needs of those above and below them in the hierarchy, and often serve as the face of leadership to many employees.

At the team level, leaders directly influence the daily experiences of individual contributors. They're tasked with motivating their teams, resolving conflicts, and ensuring that the work gets done while also developing talent and fostering a positive work environment.

Across all these levels, leadership demands a unique blend of skills, characteristics, and mindsets. It requires finesse in handling interpersonal dynamics, dedication to the mission and to the people you lead, and resilience in the face of constant challenges. These are qualities that many aspire to, but not all are willing or ready to cultivate.

My journey in the early part of my career through various leadership roles, from the receiving side in the military service to civilian management positions, serves as a stark reminder of the complexities and challenges that come with taking the helm at any level. It illustrates that leadership is not a one-size-fits-all proposition but a nuanced practice that must be adapted to the specific context, team, and organizational level in which one operates.

Being a leader, whether you're a CEO, a middle manager, or a team leader, is far more complex than simply being a boss. It's one of the most intricate roles within any organization, laden with a multitude of responsibilities, conflicting priorities, emotional complexities, and countless other challenges. As a leader at any level, you're tasked not only with guiding your direct reports to success but also with aligning your efforts with the broader organizational mission. It's a balancing act that requires strength and sensitivity, vision and attention to detail, strategic thinking, and tactical execution.

This complexity is often underestimated by those new to leadership roles, regardless of the level at which they enter. This includes CEOs. Many assume their technical expertise, past successes, or natural charisma will naturally translate into effective leadership. However, leadership at every level requires

Depth and dividends

a distinct set of skills that go beyond technical know-how or individual performance.

It involves understanding human psychology, mastering communication in various contexts, developing a strategic mindset that can navigate both short-term challenges and long-term goals, and the ability to inspire and influence others, whether you're leading a small team or an entire organization.

The ultimate goal of leadership is to serve your organization's expectations at all costs or otherwise realize that it has boundaries, and those need to be respected. But as we've learned from countless examples throughout history, and as I learned firsthand, the "big hammer" approach—ruling through force—rarely yields long-term success, and neither does complacency, hoping they will all come around. Instead, effective leadership requires a more nuanced, empathetic, and systematic approach, including a team-focused approach.

A critical military strategy you can learn from my navy experience so you can manage your team is Decentralized Command. This approach delegates decision-making authority to lower levels, fostering leadership development and quick responses. In a corporate setting, it empowers teams to address challenges promptly, and this also frees up the CEO to make the critical decisions he needs to make, rather than micro-managing every decision from the team.

As I otherwise continued to grow in leadership roles later in my career and even still today as an advisor, I realize that my actions and my ability to do the same things I was asking my team to do, over and over again, by example, was indeed the foundation of my success. This principle continues to guide me today.

I remember a very large European manufacturer that my first company represented awarded my company multiple times as the number one service organization in the Americas. As an owner, I was very proud of my team. We didn't strive for the award specifically, but what I realized was that being with my team, leading alongside them, and making myself accessible to them showed my commitment. It doesn't mean that as a CEO or an owner, you always need to be available, but what it does show—and it has proven true many times over—is that leading by example will forever create other great leaders around you and provide you, as the leader, the confidence and respect you hope to achieve to grow your business while not worrying about is my team getting it done.

As we explored the complexities of leadership in this chapter, remember that being ready to lead involves more than just willingness or past successes. It requires a nuanced understanding of human dynamics, a desire to listen and learn, and the humility to recognize when you might not have all the answers.

Leadership is not a one-size-fits-all proposition. What works in one context may fail spectacularly in another. The key is to remain adaptable, to learn and grow constantly, and to always keep the needs of your team and your organization at the forefront of your mind.

Are you indeed ready to lead?

As we conclude this exploration of leadership readiness, it's crucial to reflect on the key lessons we've uncovered. The journey of leadership, as we've seen, is fraught with challenges, but it's these very challenges that forge great leaders.

The experiences shared in this chapter – from the struggles of adapting to new leadership contexts to the humbling realization of one's unreadiness – serve as powerful reminders of the complexity inherent in leadership roles. These stories underscore a fundamental truth: leadership is not about wielding authority but about understanding, adapting, and growing.

It might help as part of this assessment to know if you are ready for something. I have included a scaling readiness checklist in Appendix I. It's primarily for the business, but you can apply it to you as a person. Are you ready to lead?

One of the most critical lessons to emerge is the importance of surrounding yourself with honest leadership. As a leader, it's tempting to surround yourself with yes-men, but proper growth comes from those who will challenge you and speak truth to power. These are the individuals who will push you to be better, to see your blind spots, and to evolve your leadership style constantly.

Equally important is the role of mentorship and advisors in leadership development. No leader, no matter how talented or experienced, can navigate the complexities of organizational leadership alone. Seeking out mentors – those who have walked the path before you – can provide invaluable insights and help you avoid pitfalls. Similarly, bringing in advisors can offer fresh perspectives and strategies that can drive your organization forward.

However, it's crucial to remember that the pursuit of growth and success can sometimes come at a cost. In the relentless drive for expansion and improvement, organizations often risk leaving behind some of their most talented individuals. These are the people who, during rapid change and mounting pressures, may not receive the attention and development they need and deserve. As a result, they may seek opportunities elsewhere, taking with them valuable skills and institutional knowledge.

This highlights a critical challenge for leaders: how to balance the demands of organizational growth with the need to nurture and retain top talent. It requires a keen awareness of your team's needs, a commitment to ongoing development at all levels, and the ability to create an environment where everyone can thrive.

As you move forward in your leadership journey, keep these lessons in mind:

- Cultivate honesty and transparency in your leadership team. Encourage open dialogue and constructive criticism.
- Actively seek mentorship, and don't hesitate to bring in advisors. Their experiences and perspectives can be invaluable in navigating complex challenges.

- Remember that leadership is context-specific. What works in one situation may not work in another. Stay adaptable and always be ready to learn.
- Pay attention to the needs of your team, especially during periods of growth or change. Don't let the pursuit of organizational goals overshadow the development and retention of your talented individuals.
- Lead by example. As we saw in the story of my award-winning service organization, your willingness to work alongside your team and remain accessible can inspire loyalty and drive success.
- Embrace failures and setbacks as learning opportunities. They are not indicators of your worth as a leader but stepping stones to becoming a better one.
- Continuously assess your readiness to lead. Leadership is not a destination but a journey of ongoing growth and development.

The path of leadership is never easy, but it is infinitely rewarding. It offers the opportunity not just to guide an organization to success but to impact the lives of those you lead positively. By staying committed to your growth, fostering an environment of honest feedback and continuous improvement, and never losing sight of the human element in leadership, you can navigate the challenges that lie ahead and truly make a difference.

As you look to the future, ask yourself: How can I create an environment where both my organization and my people can thrive? How can I ensure that in the pursuit of growth, we don't lose sight of the individuals who make that growth possible? And most importantly, how can I continue to grow and evolve as a leader to meet the ever-changing demands of my role?

Remember, authentic leadership is not about having all the answers but about having the courage to ask the right questions and the wisdom to listen to the answers. Stay curious, stay humble, and remain committed to your journey of leadership. There are many challenges ahead, but so are the opportunities to make a lasting, positive impact.

Depth and dividends

It's crucial to recognize that what we've explored here is just the crust of a much deeper, more complex conversation about leadership. The examples and insights shared are merely the starting point for our journey into understanding the intricacies of leadership across various corporate structures, multiple industries, and diverse global locations.

As we continue our exploration in the chapters to come, we'll delve into leadership roles that think and operate even more differently than what we've discussed here. We'll examine how leadership manifests in various cultural contexts around the world, each with its unique challenges and expectations. It's essential to approach these diverse leadership paradigms with an open mind, ready to learn and adapt.

Remember, effective global leadership requires not just skill and knowledge but also a deep respect for and understanding of different cultural approaches to leadership. What works in one country or industry may be ineffective or even counterproductive in another. As we explore these variations, we'll gain a richer, more nuanced understanding of what it truly means to lead in our interconnected, global business environment.

The journey ahead promises to be both challenging and enlightening. It will push us to expand our understanding of leadership beyond the familiar and comfortable, encouraging us to grow not just as leaders but as global citizens. As we embark on this continued exploration, keep an open mind and a humble heart.

The lessons we'll uncover have the power to transform not just how we lead but how we interact with and understand the diverse world around us.

So, as you reflect on the lessons from this chapter, remember: this is just the beginning. The leadership path is long and varied, with much more to discover. Stay curious, stay open, and, most importantly, remain committed to your growth as a leader. The challenges and insights that lie ahead will not only shape your leadership journey but also contribute to your understanding of our complex, diverse global business landscape.

As you move forward in your leadership journey, consider these essential lessons: How can you cultivate honesty and transparency in your leadership team, encouraging open dialogue and constructive criticism? In what ways can you actively seek mentorship and bring in advisors, leveraging their experiences and perspectives to navigate complex challenges? How will you remember that leadership is context-specific, adaptable, and always ready to learn as you face varying situations?

Consider how you can pay close attention to the needs of your team, especially during periods of growth or change. How will you ensure that the pursuit of organizational goals doesn't overshadow the development and retention of your talented individuals? Reflect on how you can lead by example, as we saw in the story of my award-winning service organization. How can your willingness to work alongside your team and remain accessible inspire loyalty and drive success?

Toolkit items you need at this stage (See Appendix I)

1. *Scaling readiness assessment.*

CHAPTER 6
WHY BUSINESSES FAIL

If you have failed before, whether in business or personally, you will likely resonate with the story Terry told - his humble pie experience when he tried to climb the corporate ladder but was cruelly brought back down. You get the drill by now; let us do a forensic analysis – I am now using an accounting term, but it is like the Navy's After-Action Reviews (AAR).

1. You notice that everything always starts well. Terry said:

> *Initially, everything seemed perfect. My new colleagues were warm and accommodating, eager to get to work.*

2. Then there is often an element of not knowing what you don't know:

> *But over time, I began to realize there was a game afoot. It wasn't malicious but rather a form of self-preservation. They knew what I didn't know, and this knowledge gap became increasingly apparent.*

3. You also notice that, despite your best efforts, you then fail:

> *After about six weeks of grinding hard and trying to build relationships, working insane hours, I was called into the owner's office. Sitting with him and his assistant of nearly 40 years, they delivered the news: I wasn't ready. They believed I had the mental and technical aptitude but lacked the necessary skill set to lead effectively in their organization.*

Depth and dividends

The narrative of Terry is sadly something I have seen over and over when I dealt with clients of all types. Terry was felled by **out-of-control growth** – meaning he bit off more than he could chew. Sadly, the narrative of why and how businesses everywhere fail is eerily similar, so in some ways, take heart – painful as this realization may be, let us now speak through the principles behind the issue of failure and how to use the knowledge of failures' fingerprints to catapult you to success.

Why businesses fail

Businesses everywhere fail for similar reasons, whether in Timbuktu, Yangon, or Wichita. A respected *New York Times* Article on the subject gives the top 10 reasons for business failure (summarised below):

1. **The math just doesn't work.** There is not enough demand for the product or service at a price that will produce a profit for the company.
2. **Owners who cannot get out of their own way.** They may be stubborn, risk-averse, or conflict-averse.
3. **Out-of-control growth.**
4. **Poor accounting.** You cannot be in control of a business if you don't know what is going on.
5. **Lack of a cash cushion.**
6. **Operational mediocrity.** Repeat and referral business is critical for most companies.
7. **Operational inefficiencies.** Paying too much for rent, labor, and materials.
8. **Dysfunctional management.** Lack of focus, vision, planning, standards, and everything else that goes into good management.
9. **The lack of a succession plan**
10. **A declining market.**

Now, there is something very critical to note about business failure that you will need to pay attention to because this topic of business failure can be very complex.

Chapter 6: Why Businesses Fail

According to a study in an emerging market, when business owners were asked to give their reasons for failure, they categorized those reasons as below:

Owners' ranking (External & internal) for business failure

1. Taxation
2. Load shedding (electricity)
3. Lack of capital
4. Poor market
5. High rent charges
6. Wrong pricing
7. Negative cash flow
8. Poor record keeping
9. Domestic and family
10. Delay in application

In the New York Times article, you will note that all reasons for failure (except no. 10) are internal and blamed on the small businesses themselves. By comparison, when the owners were asked (second study), all the top 5 reasons were blamed on external factors.

Who is correct? The author of the New York Times article rightly points out: *"One of the least understood aspects of entrepreneurship is why small businesses fail, and there's a simple reason for the confusion: Most of the evidence comes from the entrepreneurs themselves." I have had a close-up view of numerous business failures —including a few start-ups of my own. And from my observation, the reasons for failure cited by the owners are frequently off-point, which kind of makes sense when you think about it. If the owners really knew what they were doing wrong, they might have been able to fix the problem. Often, it is simply a matter of denial or of not knowing what you don't know."*

"Not knowing what you don't know" – do you recall Terry mentioning that in his later assessment?

Depth and dividends

I am therefore inclined to agree with the *New York Times* Article. While it is true that certain markets have structural challenges that are not common in, say, developed economies where, for example, electricity is a constant, roads are good, etc., I can challenge you that in whatever circumstances, true entrepreneurs rise above the challenge, and find success.

The starting point is really the market, but I shared that with you earlier when I spoke about the secrets of millionaires, so hopefully, that is no longer your problem.

Otherwise, knowledge is power, I was told when I was young. So, you should now use the knowledge of failure to "failure-proof" your business. Here are examples of how to do it now that you know the causes of business failure:

- *If you do not know how big your market is*, consider finding an expert to research and forecast.
- *If you are at risk of being rigid* – consider finding thought leadership sources of information to help challenge your thinking. Find mentors, business advisors, and others who can speak with you candidly.
- *If you are dealing with out-of-control growth* – Work with a professional such as a CPA or a fractional CFO to help you undertake cash flow forecasting to assess your future needs.
- *If you have poor accounting* – work with a professional such as a bookkeeper, accountant, CPA, or a fractional CFO to ensure you have regular management accounts and other books and records.
- *Lack of a cash cushion?* – Consider what alternative sources of finance you could assess. Might you need to work with a professional to prepare yourself for accessing this?

For homework, I leave you with the rest of the causes of business failure so you can explore how to mitigate failure with the knowledge I have given you.

I have also provided some toolkit templates in Appendix I, such as the cash flow tracker, the risk assessment template, the scaling readiness checklist, and

Chapter 6: Why Businesses Fail

the succession planning guide. Do review them to ensure you protect your business from common failures!

Special section: Does treating people well matter?

It is hard to describe business failure without dealing with the people factor. I know Terry spoke of intrigue with other team members. Still, a far more common issue is that businesses fail because many entrepreneurs treat their employees like disposable needles – to use and then throw away. This is often more common when there is a recession or similar challenging business environment such that there is high unemployment and the owner might not

Depth and dividends

worry about finding the next person. But they should watch out because this attitude gives rise to a myriad of business failure issues I highlighted earlier, for example:

- **Operational mediocrity (#6).** When mistreated, people will not care to put in the extra effort required to be excellent.
- **Operational inefficiencies (#7).** When people are mistreated, they will not care to put in the effort to help the business become more efficient.
- **Dysfunctional management (#8).** If people are mistreated, they will not help or may even sabotage the business, so it is unable to develop the focus, vision, planning, standards, and everything else that goes into good management.

But just how critical is it to treat employees well?

The Center for High Performance (CfHP) conducted a study of more than 3,000 knowledge workers around the world - the largest and most in-depth of its kind. What was found to be common worldwide for high-performing teams, whether in Idaho or Kauai, i.e., regardless of their location, industry, sector, or type of business?

Characteristics present in High Performing teams

1. People in the group feel valued
2. It is fun to be part of the group.
3. The group makes use of the highest and best talents of its employees
4. The group works to retain the best people
5. People understand how their work fits the goals of the group
6. The group leader promotes high performance by his example
7. Important information about the state of the business is shared with everyone
8. The group continually looks for ways to work more efficiently
9. Information is freely exchanged in the workgroup
10. The work group turns problems into opportunities

11. New ideas are constantly sought
12. Learning is rewarded
13. The group adapts quickly to changes in the environment
14. New ideas are tried
15. Mistakes are seen as opportunities to learn

Action point #1: Perform a diagnostic of your business. Is one of the causes of failure identified in this chapter present? If so, can you fix it? Use the risk assessment template in *Appendix I* to help you.

Action plan # 2: Valuing people is critical for success. Is your team high-performing? Ask them in a survey using the 15 characteristics highlighted and then undertake a team motivation plan using the tool in *Appendix I* to help you improve where you fall short.

As I hand you back to Terry, I feel this matter of dealing with people will be a natural bridge into his next story. In his story, you will see him moving from being an employee to an entrepreneur.

There is often a division in how an employee thinks and how an owner thinks because of the risks being taken, notably by owners – I just hope that as you make your transition, you do not forget the feeling of being an employee and how crucial it was to treat others as you wanted to be treated. I am getting philosophical – let me stop here and go to the water cooler to banter (with myself). I will see you on the high seas coming next!

Toolkit items you need at this stage (See Appendix I)

1. *cash flow tracker*
2. *the risk assessment template*
3. *the scaling readiness checklist*
4. *the succession planning guide*
5. *Team motivation plan*

CHAPTER 7
NAVIGATING THE SEAS TO ENTREPRENEURSHIP

The Seeds of Entrepreneurship

In the realm of business, there exists a natural division between leaders and followers. This distinction is not a judgment of value but rather a recognition of different roles and appetites for risk. Leaders, particularly in the entrepreneurial world, are those willing to take tremendous risks. As my career progressed, I found myself increasingly drawn to this leadership role, contemplating the leap from employee to entrepreneur.

My journey began long before I made the conscious decision to start my own business. Looking back, I can see how each experience, each interaction, and each challenge was shaping me for the path ahead. The seeds of entrepreneurship were planted early, nurtured by a combination of circumstances, mentors, and an innate desire to create something of my own.

Throughout the beginning of my career, I was fortunate to be surrounded by seasoned entrepreneurs. Some had inherited their businesses, shepherding them through generations of transition. I watched as they navigated the delicate balance of honoring tradition while driving innovation. Others had built their empires from the ground up, and their success was forged in the crucible of starting from zero. These self-made individuals showed me the power of vision, perseverance, and calculated risk-taking.

Depth and dividends

One particular mentor, let's call him Jack, left an indelible mark on my entrepreneurial mindset. Jack had started his manufacturing business in his garage, armed with nothing but an innovative product idea and unwavering determination. I remember him telling me, "Kid, the difference between a dreamer and an entrepreneur is the willingness to wake up and do the work." Jack's words stayed with me, a constant reminder that success is born from a combination of vision and relentless effort.

Learning the Ropes

My path was marked by active engagement with both customers and principal manufacturers. I took great care to understand not only the technologies and products but also the organizational structures that brought these products to market. This included a deep dive into the hierarchies of manufacturers, their use of representatives and distribution channel partners, and the strategies employed by my competitors.

You could say that to do this, I employed two military strategies.

The first is a military strategy called Center of Gravity. Identifying the 'center of gravity' refers to pinpointing the source of an opponent's strength. Applied to business, this means understanding the core strengths of competitors or one's own organization to protect and leverage them effectively.

The *second* is the OODA Loop (Observe, Orient, Decide, Act). The OODA Loop emphasizes rapid decision-making and adaptability. Applied to business, it encourages continuous observation of the market, orientation to new information, swift decision-making, and prompt action to stay ahead of competitors.

I recall a particular project where I was tasked with restructuring our distribution network. It was a complex undertaking that required me to analyze market data, negotiate with partners, and implement new systems. The process was challenging, but it gave me invaluable insights into the intricacies of business operations. I learned about the importance of building solid relationships, the power of data-driven decision-making, and the delicate art of managing change.

This hands-on experience was like a real-world MBA. Every day, I learned new lessons, from understanding financial statements to mastering the art of negotiation. I soaked it all in, not realizing at the time how crucial this knowledge would be for my future entrepreneurial endeavors.

The Turning Point

After a brief stint as a junior partner, I seriously began to contemplate my path forward. The very manufacturers and customers I worked with planted the seeds of this transition. Manufacturers would ask when I was going to "make the leap," assuring me of their support. Customers, recognizing my comprehensive approach to my territory, often remarked that I operated as though I already owned the business.

I remember one conversation vividly. It was with Sarah, a long-time client who had become a friend over the years. We were having coffee after a successful meeting, and she looked at me intently. "You know," she said, "you've outgrown this role. You're thinking like an owner, not an employee. When are you going to take the plunge and start your own thing?" Her words hit me like a thunderbolt. It was as if she had verbalized a thought that had been lurking in the back of my mind for months.

The decision to transition from employee to entrepreneur was not one I took lightly. As a young father with three amazing daughters, the responsibility of providing for my family and ensuring their security weighed heavily on my mind. This is a burden familiar to anyone contemplating such a significant career change.

I spent countless nights poring over financial projections, trying to calculate the risks and potential rewards. My wife, ever supportive, would often find me in the early hours of the morning, surrounded by spreadsheets and business plans. "Are you sure about this?" she'd ask, concern evident in her voice. I wasn't sure, not entirely. But I was sure that if I didn't try, I'd always wonder, "What if?"

Seeking Wisdom

I engaged in countless conversations with mentors and friends, receiving a mixed bag of advice. Some were enthusiastic, encouraging me to take the plunge. Others were more cautious, arguing that the risk-reward ratio didn't justify leaving the security of an established organization.

One mentor, a successful entrepreneur in his own right, gave me advice I'll never forget. "Starting a business," he said, "is like jumping off a cliff and assembling your parachute on the way down. It's terrifying, exhilarating, and the most rewarding thing you'll ever do. But make sure you have some of the pieces ready before you jump."

As I contemplated this significant change, I developed a process to guide my decision-making. This involved:

- Assessing my readiness for entrepreneurship: I took a hard look at my skills, knowledge gaps, and personal characteristics. Was I prepared for the challenges ahead? Did I have the resilience to weather the inevitable storms?
- Evaluating the market opportunity: I spent months researching the industry, identifying gaps in the market, and refining my business idea. I wanted to ensure that there was a real need for what I planned to offer.
- Considering the potential impact on my family, I had open, honest discussions with my wife about the possible risks and rewards. We talked about worst-case scenarios and how we'd handle them.
- Analyzing my financial position and risk tolerance: I took a deep dive into our finances, creating multiple scenarios to understand how long we could sustain ourselves if the business took time to become profitable.

- Identifying potential supporters and mentors: I began to build a network of advisors, reaching out to successful entrepreneurs and industry experts who could guide me on this journey.

This process, while time-consuming, gave me a clearer picture of what lay ahead. It didn't eliminate the risks but made them feel more manageable.

The Catalyst: An Unexpected Journey

Amidst this period of reflection and analysis, I had a significant encounter that would prove to be the catalyst for my entrepreneurial journey. In the aftermath of September 11th, 2001, my wife and I found ourselves with an unexpected opportunity. During a charity event, we successfully bid on a cruise to Southeast Asia and Australia. This trip, which we could hardly afford at the time, would prove to be a transformative experience that altered the trajectory of my entire career.

We arrived in Singapore, a city that seemed to embody the spirit of entrepreneurship and innovation. The energy was palpable, from the bustling streets to the gleaming skyscrapers. As we boarded the cruise ship, I was struck by its opulence. It boasted as many crew members as passengers, a testament to the level of luxury we were about to experience.

Depth and dividends

For three weeks, we found ourselves - by far the youngest couple - surrounded by some of the wealthiest individuals in the world. Their fortunes stemmed from various sources: generational wealth, entrepreneurial tenacity, and, in some cases, responses to family tragedies. It was a microcosm of the business world, filled with stories of success, failure, and everything in between.

I remember feeling out of place at first, like an imposter in a world of success and luxury. But as the days went by, I began to see beyond the surface. These weren't just wealthy individuals; they were people with stories, dreams, and their own set of challenges.

Chapter 7: Navigating the Seas to Entrepreneurship

Lessons from the Sea

Throughout the cruise, I had countless opportunities to engage in relaxed conversations with these remarkable men and women. While some exuded arrogance, others impressed me with their humility and zest for life. Each interaction was a lesson, a glimpse into the mindset of those who had achieved great success.

One conversation stands out in particular. It was with a woman who had built a tech empire from scratch. As we stood at the ship's railing, watching the sunset over the South China Sea, she shared her philosophy on success. "The secret," she said, "is to fall in love with the problem, not the solution. The world changes too fast for any single solution to last. But if you're obsessed with solving a real problem, you'll always find a way."

Her words struck a chord. I realized that my passion wasn't just for the products I sold or the industry I worked in. It was for solving problems, for making things work better. This realization would later shape the very foundation of my business approach.

But the most impactful encounter was yet to come. One gentleman, in particular, left an indelible mark on my journey. I would often find him in the ship's humidor, peacefully gazing out at the open ocean. After a few days, I mustered the courage to strike up a conversation. His warm smile and invitation to join him led to eight or nine more hour-long discussions throughout the cruise.

This man, an African American real estate tycoon from Chicago, shared his life story - from his childhood struggles to his remarkable success in a field where many thought it impossible for someone of his background. His journey was a testament to perseverance, innovation, and the power of self-belief.

In turn, I opened up about my family history, career thus far, and naivety about the "real world." Our conversations deepened over time, becoming increasingly personal. I peppered him with questions about his journey: How did he do it? When? Why? What drove him to such success?

His answers were never what I expected. He didn't focus on strategies or business models. Instead, he spoke about values, about staying true to oneself in the face of adversity. "Success," he told me, "is not about the deals you close or the money you make. It's about the impact you have on the lives you touch. Everything else is just a byproduct."

The Moment of Truth

Around our fifth or sixth meeting, he asked why I hadn't considered starting my own business. The question caught me off guard. I confided in him about my anxieties - the fear of failure, concerns about my family's security, and the capital needed to start and maintain a business. We discussed the intricacies of my industry, its challenges, and the dynamics of entrepreneurship.

He listened patiently, nodding as I laid out all my concerns. When I finished, he was quiet for a moment, puffing on his cigar and gazing out at the horizon. Then he turned to me with a look of understanding mixed with challenge.

"Let me ask you something," he said. "What's the worst that could happen if you fail?"

I started to list off all the potential disasters - financial ruin, letting down my family, damaging my professional reputation. He held up his hand to stop me.

"Now, what's the worst that could happen if you don't try?"

That question hit me like a ton of bricks. I realized that the regret of not taking this chance, of always wondering "what if," was far more terrifying than any potential failure.

In our final conversation, he posed a simple yet profound question: "What is stopping you?" He gestured around the ship, saying, "Look at the wealth on this boat. Is this what you strive for? Because if it is, you've accomplished it.

Now be humble, go back, start a business. Thrive in your business. Take risks in your business."

This conversation was the catalyst I needed. I returned to our stateroom, brimming with excitement, and told my wife, "That's it. I'm going home to start my business." Despite not fully grasping what this meant, my confidence was soaring.

The Journey Home

As we flew back from Singapore to Portland, Maine, a whirlwind of emotions and thoughts consumed me. What exactly would I do? How would I start? Like any family facing a significant life change, my wife expressed concerns about our children's well-being and our ability to meet our financial obligations. Yet, the seed had been planted. The wealth of knowledge shared by my unexpected mentor, combined with the unique perspective gained from this extraordinary trip, had set me on an irreversible path toward entrepreneurship.

The stark contrast between the luxury of the cruise and the uncertainty of my future was not lost on me. As our plane descended into the familiar landscape of Maine, I felt a mixture of excitement and trepidation. The comfortable life I had known was about to change dramatically.

Taking the Leap

Following the transformative experience at sea, I found myself at a crossroads. The frustration with my current partnership had reached a boiling point, and I knew it was time to make a change. The dysfunctional relationship with my partner had become untenable, pushing me towards the decision to venture out on my own.

As I contemplated this significant step, I reflected on the years of encouragement I had received from various quarters. Customers had long been urging me to strike out on my own, often questioning why I hadn't

Depth and dividends

taken the leap earlier. Their faith in my abilities and potential had been a constant, albeit unrealized, source of motivation.

Interestingly, as I stood on the precipice of this major life change, fear of failure was conspicuously absent from my thoughts. Instead, my mind was filled with visions of the future and the hard work that lay ahead. I recognized the challenges I would face, but I also acknowledged the hard work I had already invested to reach this point - work that had earned me the respect and encouragement of those around me.

It's a curious symmetry that the sea played such a significant role in both the beginning and the turning point of my career. I began my professional life under the water, and now I was making the most significant change in my career journey on top of the water at sea. This parallel wasn't lost on me, and it seemed to imbue my decision with a sense of destiny.

The decision, which had been brewing in my mind throughout the cruise and in the weeks following my return, was now crystal clear. I had made up my mind. The only thing left was to execute my plan.

The First Steps

Upon returning home after leaving my position, I faced the daunting task of explaining my decision to my wife. As news of my departure spread, my ex-partner focused on securing his business, not realizing I had no intention to harm it but rather to seize my own opportunity as an entrepreneur.

Amidst the chaos, customers began calling, notably a cherished mentor and procurement manager from a large pulp and paper company in the Northeast. His questions about whether I have a basement office or a company name caught me off guard, highlighting how unprepared I indeed was. The persistent inquiries from customers and manufacturers forced me to confront whether I had left to start a business or merely out of frustration.

Chapter 7: Navigating the Seas to Entrepreneurship

After a few days of reflection, I took a leap of faith and contacted the bank to discuss a business loan. With a company name in mind, I was ready for the next step, but like all startups, funding was a critical concern. I had home equity, a family to support, and a lifestyle to maintain at least a minimum.

My conversation with an old-school banker led to a challenge: create a business plan in a week. Despite never having written one before, I sought advice from friends and business acquaintances to craft a comprehensive plan. I spent sleepless nights researching, writing, and refining my ideas. It was a crash course in business planning, forcing me to think through every aspect of my proposed venture.

During our meeting in my family room, the banker focused on the commitment of my industry relationships. Fortunately, I had purchase orders in hand and more waiting, proving my viability. This tangible evidence of market demand was crucial in securing the initial funding I needed.

This marked the beginning of my first company, Allagash Valve and Controls. The name was a nod to the Allagash River in Maine, symbolizing the flow and control that our products would provide. It was a testament to the power of relationships, preparation, and the courage to take that crucial first step into entrepreneurship.

The Early Days of Allagash Valve and Controls

The early days of Allagash were a whirlwind of activity. Setting up shop in my family room, I found myself wearing multiple hats - salesman, accountant, inventory manager, and sometimes even delivery person. Every day brought new challenges and learning opportunities.

I remember the first order we received. It was a relatively small one, but the sense of accomplishment was immense. As I packaged the products myself, carefully labeling each item, I felt pride. This wasn't just a sale; it was the first tangible proof that my dream was becoming a reality.

Depth and dividends

But with the highs came the lows. There were sleepless nights worrying about cash flow, days when I questioned my decision, and moments when the sheer volume of work seemed overwhelming. Yet, each challenge overcame and each problem solved added to my growing confidence and expertise.

One particular incident stands out. A crucial shipment to a major client was delayed due to a supplier issue. The client was upset and threatened to cancel not just this order but all future business. I spent 48 hours straight working on a solution, coordinating with suppliers, arranging alternative shipping, and personally driving part of the order to the client's facility. In the end, not only did we save the order, but the client was so impressed with our dedication that they increased their business with us.

This experience taught me valuable lessons about problem-solving, the importance of building solid relationships with both clients and suppliers, and the power of going above and beyond to exceed expectations. It became a cornerstone of Allagash's customer service philosophy.

As the business grew, so did the challenges. Managing inventory became increasingly complex. I learned the hard way about the delicate balance between having enough stock to meet demand and not tying up too much capital in inventory. There were times when I had to take out personal loans to cover payroll or keep the lights on. These were humbling experiences, but they taught me the importance of careful financial management and planning.

One of the most significant challenges was building a team. As orders increased, I couldn't handle everything on my own anymore. Hiring my first employee was a momentous occasion. I remember feeling a mix of excitement and trepidation. This person was entrusting their livelihood to my vision, and I felt the weight of that responsibility as a family member.

Over time, I learned to delegate, trust in the abilities of others, and focus on building a company culture that reflected my values of integrity, hard work, and customer focus. Each new hire brought new perspectives and skills to the table, helping Allagash grow in ways I hadn't anticipated.

Lessons Learned and Reflections

The time spent at sea proved to be more than just a luxurious getaway; it was a profound learning experience that shaped my entrepreneurial journey. The most impactful aspect was my interactions with the gentleman who became an unexpected mentor. His words resonated deeply: "This is the best it gets. If this is what everybody strives to see, you'll come to realize this is it."

As I observed my fellow passengers, I realized we were all eating the same food, sleeping in similar beds, and sharing the same cruise experience. The only differences were in degrees of wealth and personal circumstances. Some were there to escape, like the individual whose family had been dramatically affected by the September 11th tragedy. This realization led me to question: If this is what everyone is pushing for, and I've already experienced it, why become an entrepreneur?

It was during this time that I formulated a personal mantra that has guided me for the past 25 years: "I love what I do, and by default, I make good money at it." This simple yet profound statement encapsulates my approach to entrepreneurship and career satisfaction. It's not about chasing wealth for its own sake but about finding fulfillment in your work and allowing success to follow naturally.

As an aspiring entrepreneur, I came to understand the importance of clearly defining one's motivations. What does one genuinely want to achieve through entrepreneurship? Is it driven by vanity, a desire to contribute to society, financial gain, or a combination of these factors? Each motivation is valid, but they must be balanced and understood.

For me, the drive came from a desire to solve problems to create value for customers in ways that larger, less flexible companies couldn't. I wanted to

Depth and dividends

build something that would outlast me, that would provide opportunities for others, and contribute positively to my industry and community.

The early stages of putting a business together, particularly facing tough financial questions from the bank, brought home the magnitude of the decision I was making. While the initial months of entrepreneurship can seem manageable – with orders trickling in and finances under control – the real challenges emerge as success grows and the business expands.

I learned that success often brings its own set of problems. As Allagash grew, I had to navigate new challenges: scaling operations, managing a growing team, dealing with larger competitors, and maintaining the quality and customer focus that had been our hallmark. Each stage of growth required a different set of skills, forcing me to continually learn and adapt.

One particularly valuable lesson was the importance of building a strong network. I found mentors in unexpected places – from industry veterans to young tech entrepreneurs who taught me about emerging technologies that could benefit our business. I learned to value diverse perspectives and sought advisors, sometimes even at a hefty fee.

Another crucial realization was the importance of work-life balance. In the early days, I worked around the clock, often at the expense of family time and personal health. It took a wake-up call – missing an important milestone in my daughter's life – to make me reassess my priorities. I learned that being a successful entrepreneur doesn't mean sacrificing everything else. In fact, maintaining balance made me a better leader and decision-maker. Don't get me wrong, I still struggle with this today, as all entrepreneurs do.

The Evolution of Allagash and Personal Growth

As Allagash Valve and Controls grew from a basement startup to a respected player in the industry, I found myself evolving as well. The brash confidence of my early entrepreneurial days gave way to a more measured, strategic approach. I learned to value patience, to think long-term, and to build sustainable practices into every aspect of the business.

One of the most rewarding aspects of this journey has been watching employees grow with the company. Seeing someone I hired as an entry-level worker rise to a leadership position or helping a team member start their own venture brings a sense of fulfillment that's hard to describe. It reinforced my belief that a truly successful business creates value not just for customers and shareholders but for employees and the broader community as well.

There were, of course, setbacks along the way. Economic downturns, loss of key clients, and technological disruptions all posed significant challenges. Each crisis tested our resilience and forced us to innovate. I remember one particularly difficult period during the 2008 financial crisis. Orders dried up almost overnight, and we had to make tough decisions to keep the company afloat.

It was during this time that the actual value of the relationships we'd built over the years became apparent. Loyal customers stick with us, sometimes even prepaying orders to help with our cash flow. Suppliers extended credit terms. These gestures of support were humbling and reinforced the importance of integrity and relationship-building in business.

Coming out of that crisis, we emerged stronger, more efficient, and with a clearer sense of our core values and mission. It was a powerful reminder that adversity, while painful, often carries the seeds of future growth and improvement.

Reflections for the Aspiring and Practicing Entrepreneur

As we conclude this chapter on the transition from employee to entrepreneur, it's crucial to pause and reflect. Whether you're considering entrepreneurship, in the early stages of your venture, or an established

Depth and dividends

business owner, these reflections will help you analyze your journey and realign with your core values and motivations.

For Start-ups: Understanding Your Entrepreneurial Drive

Begin by examining your primary motivation for becoming an entrepreneur. Is it financial independence, a desire to solve a specific problem or fill a market gap, the freedom to make your own decisions, or a need for personal growth and challenge? Consider how entrepreneurship aligns with your personal values and life goals. Does running your own business contribute to your ideal work-life balance? In what ways does entrepreneurship allow you to express your creativity or expertise?

Reflect on how being an entrepreneur fits into your long-term vision for your life. Take stock of the unique skills, experiences, or perspectives you bring to entrepreneurship. How can these attributes give you a competitive edge in your chosen field? Are there areas where you need to develop new skills or knowledge?

Remember, there's no one-size-fits-all approach to entrepreneurship. Your personal experiences, skills, and vision will uniquely shape your journey. Embrace this uniqueness – it's what will set you apart in a crowded marketplace.

This is the point where you might wish to consider using the initial toolkits, which I include in Appendix I to help you put together your plan:

1. Start-up budget
2. Break-even analysis worksheet
3. Tax planning basics

For Growing Companies: Evaluating Your Entrepreneurial Journey

For those already on the entrepreneurial path, reflecting on your initial reasons for starting your business is essential. Have they changed over time? If so, how have they evolved, and why? Are your current actions and decisions still aligned with these reasons?

Consider how well you're balancing the various aspects of entrepreneurship: financial success, personal fulfillment, impact on your industry or community, and work-life balance. Reflect on the ways entrepreneurship has challenged your expectations. What has been easier or more complicated than you anticipated? How have you grown or changed as a person since becoming an entrepreneur?

It's easy to get caught up in the day-to-day operations of your business and lose sight of the bigger picture. Regular reflection can help you stay true to your vision and values, even as your business evolves. Are you surrounding yourself with mentors and advisors that challenge you? "What do you want to be when you grow up?"

This question I ask even the most seasoned entrepreneurs that we advise today.

An annual review checklist (*Appendix I*) helps you take stock and be able to answer this question.

Additionally, this is the point where you might wish to continue to improve your deal-making skills, so consider the following tool kits (*Appendix 1*):

1. Negotiation prep sheet
2. Deal comparison matrix

Critical Insight #1: Building and Maintaining a Supportive Network

Think about the key advisors and mentors in your entrepreneurial journey. How diverse is this group in terms of expertise and perspectives? Are there gaps in your support network that need to be filled fractionally or in the interim as you look more closely at growth? Consider how often you seek advice or feedback from others. Are you open to constructive criticism and new ideas? How do you balance taking advice with trusting your instincts?

> *One of my favorite quotes is, "Experience isn't the best teacher... other people's experience is."*
>
> **-Andy Andrew**

Reflect on the ways you give back to the entrepreneurial community. Are you mentoring others or sharing your experiences? How does this contribute to your growth and satisfaction?

Remember, entrepreneurship can be a lonely journey, but it doesn't have to be. Building a solid network of mentors, peers, and advisors can provide crucial support, fresh perspectives, and opportunities for growth.

Critical Insight #2: Staying True to Your Entrepreneurial Purpose

Take time to revisit your original business plan or vision statement. How closely does your current business align with your initial vision? What adjustments have you made, and were they necessary pivots or distractions? Define your measure of success. Is it purely financial, or do other factors play a role? How often do you reassess and adjust your definition of success?

Consider how you maintain focus on your core mission when faced with new opportunities or challenges. What strategies do you use to evaluate potential changes to your business? How do you balance staying true to your original purpose with the need for innovation and adaptation?

In my experience, the most successful entrepreneurs are those who remain flexible in their strategies but unwavering in their core purpose and values.

Critical Insight #3: Looking to the Future

As you look ahead, consider your long-term goals for your business. How do these align with your personal goals and values? What steps are you taking now to work towards these goals? Reflect on how you're preparing for future challenges and opportunities. Are you staying informed about industry trends and technological advancements? How are you developing your skills and those of your team?

Finally, consider what legacy you hope to leave as an entrepreneur. How does this influence your day-to-day decisions and long-term strategy?

The business landscape is constantly changing. Successful entrepreneurs are those who can anticipate changes, adapt quickly, and see opportunities where others see obstacles.

By regularly engaging in this type of reflection, you can ensure that your entrepreneurial journey remains true to your values and continues to fulfill your personal and professional goals, which allows you to make a meaningful impact in your chosen field.

Remember, entrepreneurship is not just about building a successful business but about creating a life that aligns with your deepest aspirations and allows you to contribute your unique gifts to the world.

As you progress in your entrepreneurial journey, let these reflections guide you, challenge you, and inspire you to grow continually and evolve both as a business owner and an individual.

The path of entrepreneurship is rarely easy, but for those who are called to it, it can be one of the most rewarding journeys imaginable.

Remember, your entrepreneurial journey is uniquely yours. Embrace the challenges, celebrate the successes, learn from the failures, and always stay true to the vision that inspired you to take that first bold step into the world of entrepreneurship.

Toolkit items you need at this stage (See Appendix I)

1. *Start-up budget*
2. *Break-even analysis worksheet*
3. *Tax planning basics*
4. *Annual review checklist*
5. *Negotiation prep sheet*
6. *Deal comparison matrix*

CHAPTER 8
HOW TO GET ALL THE FUNDING YOU NEED

The secret truth that brings unlimited funding

I am hoping that as I help you analyze the case study of Terry's journey from Submariner to Entrepreneur, you can start to see specific patterns that will be repeatable during your journey. Let me test you:

1. If you want to grow - sell more like the millionaires (Chapter 4).
2. If you do not want to fail in business – solve the #1 issue, the market issue (Chapter 6).
3. If you want to get all the funding you need…..

The answer is "have the market." It is all about the market, baby. Can I call you that? (#wokewars). Anyway, notice what Terry said when he was getting ready to become an entrepreneur:

> *My conversation with an old-school banker led to a challenge: create a business plan in a week. Despite never having written one before, I sought advice from friends and business acquaintances to craft a comprehensive plan. I spent sleepless nights researching, writing, and refining my ideas. It was a crash course in business planning, forcing me to think through every aspect of my proposed venture.*
>
> *During our meeting in my family room, the banker <u>focused</u> on the commitment of my industry relationships. Fortunately, I had purchase*

> *orders in hand and more waiting, proving my viability. This tangible evidence of market demand was crucial in securing the initial funding I needed."*

If you mull over just those few sentences, especially focusing on what the banker friend wanted to see, you will realize that whether the banker is your friend or foe, to get ALL the funding you require, you need:

1. A good business plan (or pitch deck).
2. Proof of market viability.

This is what I will now help you to understand in more detail.

What exactly do lenders care about?

In business, you will most likely need to apply for a loan or seek financing from a 3rd party. Yes, I know I said in *Chapter Two* that one of the principles is that you should try not to borrow, but sometimes it is inevitable. Assuming you MUST borrow, there are several things to know from the lenders' perspective. For example, in The Art of War, a book on military strategy, author Sun Tzu says: "Know your enemy."

Most people do not know what the lenders are looking for or how to raise additional funding/capital. So, they are often left shocked when they cannot raise additional capital for their business despite having, in their view, "a brilliant idea."

Over several years, I have reviewed the typical funding requirements of more than 20 financiers of different types, including:

- **Venture Capital (VC) Firms** - This is funding available primarily for startup companies. The venture capitalist usually takes a % of shares (instead of collateral) and expects to exit in 5-7 years from the company.
- **Private Equity (PE).** This funding is available primarily for established businesses to grow to the next level. The private equity

Chapter 8: How To Get All The Funding You Need

fund also takes a % of shares but might offer debt or a combination of debt and equity.
- **Traditional lenders** (e.g., banks, leasing companies, and through bodies like the *SBA*).
- **Grant providers** such as grants.gov, grant watch, Candid, or *Foundation Directory* online.

When I studied their requirements, a few common trends emerged.

The following are the key considerations from the lenders I researched and my experience with multiple clients seeking funding.

Scalable market

This is the first key issue lenders care about, just like it was for Terry's banker friend (meaning the traditional lenders). It is also the same for alternative lenders (e.g., VC and PE). VC and PE financiers are looking to profit from their shares in your company should it turn out to be the next big thing (like, say, Nvidia, Google, or Facebook). They want to get, say, 5x or 10x their investment, and to get this kind of return, they need to be sure that your market is big.

Scalable means that if the concept/idea works in South Florida, it can be repeated/rolled out in, say, North Carolina, London, and East Africa. For example, Mobile Money in East Africa and its US equivalents - *Cash App or Zelle*.

In Terry's case, he proved he already had orders in hand. This is a great starting point to confirm the viability of your market. In other cases, as you build your business plan, you can prove this market differently, such as by selling sample products. Concentrate on this first and foremost in your business plan and as you build your concept.

Team

This is often the second most significant issue for any lender. For the lender, it is critical that the borrower's team is experienced, ambitious, and has the vision to implement the strategy they speak of in the business plan. This means that if you are to put together your business plan, you need to clearly put together a robust and balanced team with sufficient experience. One that will convince lenders that the idea will work successfully and the team knows what it is doing (and where it's going).

If you do not have all the necessary skills in-house, consider a fractional leader to augment your team.

Corporate governance

Terry did not directly mention this, but corporate governance is critical as your business becomes riskier or more complex. What is Corporate Governance? Put simply: "It is the process by which the company's management is being monitored by someone else." For example, it is the process of having a board of directors to set the framework and to whom management is accountable.

Why is this stuff important for the lenders/financiers?

In many cases, there is a direct correlation between companies failing (failing to take off, making losses, winding up) and not implementing proper checks and balances. Many of the causes of failure I mentioned in *Chapter 6* can be fixed by having a sound corporate governance system in place, and I will cover that a bit more later.

Additionally, these lenders themselves are often supported by institutional investors, pension funds, government bodies, international lenders (like IMF), and other backers who need to be sure that the entity they are investing in is running the business properly with checks and balances like board of directors' meetings, an independent non-executive, regular accounts, and regular internal control checks.

All the largest and most successful companies have strong corporate governance. So likewise, these lenders expect that before they part with their hard-earned money, you will have corporate governance in place, especially as you scale.

Audited accounts

Audited accounts are also increasingly critical as you scale your business because it goes without saying that typically, for you to get 3rd party funding, they will expect to see your books of accounts, as independently checked by an auditor (a particular type of accountant), notably as the amounts they lend you increase.

Auditors in the US are sometimes referred to as public accountants, but auditors are also CPAs by qualification. If you are curious, I am a CPA who specializes in auditing. But you don't really care about me; it's all about the Benjamins baby, right? Well, let us move on swiftly, with no hard feelings (*#wokerevolutionreloaded*).

Why are audited accounts important?

The lenders are investing their money (or other people's money), so they need to reasonably satisfy themselves that you are giving them the "real deal." Many of these lenders will expect at least 3 years of audited results (hopefully profitable). The more reputable your auditor, the higher the chance they will take you at your word and fund you.

Ethics and Social Impact

Financiers are increasingly conscious about whether the business will act responsibly; hence, Environmental, Social, and Governance (ESG) factors are increasingly important. Nothing damages a business' fortunes like bad publicity from unethical practices (such as using harmful chemicals in agriculture). Information travels quickly via X (formerly Twitter), TikTok, Facebook, and other social media platforms. Therefore, your business plans must clearly show how your business will first do no harm to the community but will also, importantly, be impactful – in your local community and for the planet.

A recap (aka what this means for you)

How can you use the knowledge of what lenders look for to ensure that your enterprise will be better prepared for additional capital when you put together your business plan? Some of the example points I mentioned are:

- *Scalable market/team/ESG impact* - ensure your business plan or pitch deck and the supporting documents clearly show your strategies for scaling your market, meeting ESG requirements, and showcasing in detail the excellent team who will pull this off!
- *Corporate governance* - ensure you have a board of directors in place and that regular meetings are taking place where you discuss risk management, accounts, and other vital matters.
- *Audited accounts* - find a CPA or public accounting firm to audit the business. Typically, think in advance as you usually need up to 3 years of audited books when the time comes.

If you can address the above insights I have shared, starting with solving the market issue, you will get all the funding you need until you tell the lenders to stop throwing money at you!

You will likely need professional help to pull this off, especially if you do not have Terry's warm introduction from his old school banker friend or if you do not have experienced mentors and contacts as he did. This is critical because investors will not part with their hard-earned cash if you do not even try to get it right. They can likely spot amateurish effort compared to documents a professional has seen. Can you afford to blow a once-in-a-lifetime opportunity?

Do not, however, let all the hard work almost kill you, literally, as we are going to find out in the following critical story from Terry. Stay well (literally).

Toolkit items you need at this stage (See Appendix I)

1. *Cash flow tracker*
2. *Break-even analysis worksheet*
3. *Compliance checklist*
4. *Scaling readiness checklist*
5. *Risk assessment template*
6. *Deal comparison matrix*
7. *Funding Decision Matrix*

CHAPTER 9
THE SILENT SHIFT - TURNING INWARD

Success in entrepreneurship often comes with an unexpected price tag - one that isn't measured in dollars and cents but in fundamental changes to who we are and how we interact with the world. The journey from being an outgoing, problem-solving force of nature to finding yourself increasingly turned inward is a transformation few entrepreneurs discuss openly, yet most experience deeply.

I learned this lesson the hard way on a crisp fall day in northern Maine at a paper mill where the autumn air carried both the sharp scent of pine and the heavy responsibility of problems waiting to be solved. As always, I was there to help - it's what entrepreneurs do, after all. We solve problems. Sometimes our customers' problems. Sometimes our employees have issues. Often, we take on these challenges as if they were our own, carrying them with us like extra weights in an already heavy seabag.

The pulp mill manager had called about issues with a crucial piece of equipment. Thirteen flights of stairs stood between us and the problem area - a vertical challenge I'd generally tackle without a second thought. After climbing up for the initial inspection and returning down to discuss solutions with the engineering team, something nagged me. I'd missed something. I needed another look.

Depth and dividends

Halfway up those stairs the second time, my body decided to send me a message I couldn't ignore. I found myself on my knees, a crushing pressure in my chest that shouldn't have been there, ten stores up. Not at my age. Not with my energy level. Not with all the things I still needed to accomplish that day.

The entrepreneur in me - the problem solver, the never-show-weakness leader - tried to brush it off.

I made my way back down to the plant office, telling the management team not to worry; I'd just grab something at McDonald's. They looked at me and laughed, but not because anything was funny. These were dear friends who could see what I couldn't - or wouldn't - acknowledge. Their concerned faces and knowing looks should have been a warning sign, but I wasn't hearing myself, let alone them. Terry, we are calling the ambulance. I was determined to just get a bite to eat, but on my way, I realized I was not hungry.

The drive to the local hospital wasn't my wisest decision. Still, it was typically entrepreneurial - handling things myself and staying in control even when control was the last thing I had. The moment I walked into the emergency room and described my symptoms, everything changed. Before I could even finish explaining, I was whisked onto a gurney and suddenly found myself racing through a labyrinth of corridors and rooms, medical staff moving with an urgency that finally made me realize this wasn't just exhaustion or missed meals.

What I thought would be a quick check turned into a three-day ordeal. The medical team refused to let me leave, running test after test, and their concern was evident in their thoroughness. After multiple rounds of diagnostics and a complete heart catheterization procedure, I found myself looking up at my doctor as he asked a deceptively simple question: "When was the last time you really went on vacation?" then his following words were, "Your heart is as healthy as a bull."

Chapter 9: The Silent Shift - Turning Inward

The silence that followed his question was deafening. I couldn't remember. Years had passed in a blur of raising a family, customer meetings, problem-solving sessions, family gatherings that weren't quite vacations, and the constant push forward that defines entrepreneurial life. I had been so focused on maintaining the outward appearance of the confident, energetic business leader that I'd completely lost touch with my inner balance.

A Turning Point

This experience in Maine proved to be more than just a health scare - it was a life-changing moment for me as an entrepreneur. To say it scared the hell out of me would be an understatement. With a wife and three children at home, I was forced to confront a harsh reality: I couldn't let this happen again. The weight of responsibility I felt as a business leader was significant, but the commitment to my family was paramount.

The experience fundamentally changed how I approached life in general. I took that vacation the doctor recommended - my first real break in years. But more importantly, I became more cognizant of the warning signs my body and mind were sending me.

The transformation from extrovert to introvert wasn't complete, and there were still many challenges ahead, but now I was aware. Aware of the costs of ignoring these signals, mindful of the need for balance, and aware that being a successful entrepreneur meant being around long enough to see that success flourish.

Yet, this was just the beginning of my journey to understanding the delicate balance between driving business success and maintaining personal well-being. There was still much more to come, more lessons to learn, and more challenges to face. But this moment in Maine served as a crucial waypoint - a clear marker between the entrepreneur I had been and the one I needed to become.

The Unexpected Transformation

The shift from extrovert to introvert in entrepreneurship isn't a simple personality change - it's a complex transformation that affects every aspect of how we operate. It's a shift that happens in distinct layers, each bringing its own challenges and requiring its own type of balance.

As entrepreneurs, our minds never indeed shut off. What starts as energetic problem-solving and creative thinking can slowly transform into a constant internal dialogue of worry and responsibility. Where we once thrived on brainstorming sessions and collaborative meetings, we increasingly find ourselves seeking solitude to process the countless decisions that rest solely on our shoulders.

I remember sitting in my office late one night, long after everyone else had gone home, staring at spreadsheets that would determine the future of several families' livelihoods. At that moment, I realized that the gregarious person who once fed off group energy had been replaced by someone who needed solitude to carry the weight of such decisions.

The change in how we interact with others is often the most noticeable aspect of this transformation. Entrepreneurs typically start their journey as natural networkers - the life of industry events, comfortable in any room, ready to engage with anyone who might help advance their vision; this was fully me. But as the business grows, something subtle begins to change.

The same events that once energized us start to feel draining. Small talk becomes an effort rather than a pleasure. We find ourselves calculating the Return On Investment (ROI) of every social interaction, not because we've become cold or uncaring, but because the weight of responsibility has changed how we value and spend our energy.

The Leadership Paradox

Perhaps the most challenging aspect of this transformation is maintaining the appearance of the confident, outgoing leader while processing an increasingly complex internal world. It's what I call the "leadership paradox" - the need to be both more visible and more introspective as your business grows.

Your team needs to see you as the steady, approachable figure at the helm. Your clients need to feel your enthusiasm and engagement. Your partners need to sense your confidence and drive. Yet internally, you're processing more information, handling more stress, and carrying more responsibility.

The Reality of Constant Thoughts

What few people outside the entrepreneurial world understand is the perpetual nature of our mental engagement. It's not just about working long hours - it's about the constant stream of thoughts that accompany us everywhere. At dinner with family, during a child's softball game, or in those quiet moments before dawn, our minds are processing, planning, and problem-solving.

I remember sitting at one of my daughter's school plays, physically present but mentally calculating cash flow projections. The guilt of that moment still resonates - not just because I wasn't fully present, but because I recognized a pattern that had become all too common. The natural extrovert in me, who once lived fully in each moment, had been replaced by someone constantly pulled into internal dialogue.

The Price of Perpetual Processing

This constant mental engagement extracts a toll that manifests in various ways. The physical symptoms we rationalize away become more frequent and more complex to ignore. The emotional distance from those closest to us grows wider, even as we tell ourselves it's temporary. We experience a decreased ability to enjoy simple pleasures, finding our minds wandering to business concerns during what should be moments of relaxation.

Perhaps most ironically, we find ourselves caught in the paradox of being busier but feeling less productive. The more our minds race, the less effective we become at actually solving problems. It's like trying to listen to multiple radio stations at once - eventually, all you hear is noise.

I've seen fellow entrepreneurs fall into this trap, pushing themselves to the brink of exhaustion while insisting they're "fine." We wear our constant business like a badge of honor, not realizing that this perpetual processing is actually diminishing our effectiveness as leaders and decision-makers.

Learning to Navigate the New Normal

The transformation from extrovert to introvert isn't something to cure - it's something to manage. It's a natural evolution that comes with the territory of building and running a successful business. The key lies not in resisting this change but in developing strategies to navigate it effectively.

Just as we schedule meetings and block time for essential tasks, we must deliberately create space for mental processing. This isn't the same as traditional work-life balance; it's about finding equilibrium within our own minds. Some strategies that have worked for me include:

- Designated "thinking time" where interruptions are not allowed
- Regular physical exercise that enables the mind to process subconsciously, with ZERO connectivity
- Structured breaks from decision-making
- Intentional moments of complete disconnection
- Creating boundaries between work thoughts and personal time
- Learning when to engage our extroverted side and when to honor our need for introspection becomes crucial.

This isn't about becoming a hermit; it's about being strategic with our social energy. Success lies in understanding which interactions truly require our presence and which can be delegated or approached differently.

The Power of Selective Engagement

As entrepreneurs, we must learn to be selective about where and how we expend our social energy. This means:

- Choosing which meetings truly require our presence
- Delegating social responsibilities when appropriate
- Maintaining critical relationships while setting clear boundaries
- Finding environments that energize rather than drain us
- Recognizing when we need to step back and recharge

The goal isn't to withdraw completely but to engage more purposefully. When we do choose to be present in social situations, we can bring our total energy and attention, making those interactions more meaningful and productive.

Understanding the Signals

Our bodies and minds send us signals long before we reach a crisis point. The challenge is learning to recognize and respect these signals rather than pushing through them. Some common indicators include:

- Unusual physical fatigue after social interactions
- Increased irritability in group settings
- A strong urge to solve problems alone rather than collaboratively
- Physical symptoms that seem unrelated to any specific cause
- Changes in sleep patterns or quality
- Difficulty focusing during social interactions
- A growing sense of emotional disconnection

The difference between successful adaptation and potential crisis often lies in how we respond to these early warning signs. It's not about weakness; it's about wisdom in recognizing and respecting our limits.

Finding Your Path to Balance - A Personal Journey

I remember a conversation with one of my longtime executive assistants that really struck home. She pulled me aside one day and said, "You know, we all see it. You come in early, stay late, and solve everyone's problems. But lately, your eyes look tired. Not just tired - distant." It was a wake-up call that even as I thought I was mastering this balancing act, others could see what I was missing.

That's the thing about being a leader - all eyes are always on you, but not just in the way you might think. Yes, they're watching how you handle decisions and challenges, but they're also watching how you're handling yourself. The weight of their concern can sometimes feel heavier than the weight of their expectations. Over the years, I've come to realize that staying active physically is a critical component of resetting not only your biological clock but your mental clock as well.

The relentless stresses of entrepreneurship don't have to define you. Yes, they'll always be there, but you can learn to navigate them without sacrificing your health, your relationships, or your joy in the journey. It's imperative that you find mentors or advisors to stand by you and consult with people outside of your family structure. Many times, people asked why I would pull over to the side of the road at the end of the day when I was only half a mile from home and had just sat there for 30 minutes. It was to try to disengage.

I discovered my salvation in the most unexpected places. My Old Town canoe became my sanctuary. Over the years, one of the joys I came to realize was looking at the environment that was around me. I remember vividly having that Old Town canoe on top of the pickup truck that I used to drive. So, at the end of the day, when I was traveling in Maine or the northern New

Chapter 9: The Silent Shift - Turning Inward

England states, I would find a lake or a pond and put the canoe in with a fishing pole to calm my mind.

I remember one evening at Chimney Pond, Baxter State Park. The sun was setting, my fishing line was in the water (though I wasn't really fishing), and for the first time in weeks, my mind wasn't racing through profit margins and project deadlines.

Instead, I was watching a pair of loons dive for their dinner, listening to the wind in the pines along the shore. It sounds almost too simple, doesn't it? But in that moment, I found what every entrepreneur desperately needs - perspective.

It truly became an amazing type of calmness and reflection of my blessings that allowed me to relax, at the same time processing things clearly, calmly, and concisely so that when I would have a conversation at home with friends, I was relaxed.

That half-mile stop before home that I mentioned became a ritual. I'd pull over at a quiet spot overlooking the water near my house. Sometimes I'd sit there for 15 minutes, sometimes for an hour. My family had no idea; it was about ensuring that when I walked through the door, I was truly present. It was about transitioning from being the entrepreneur everyone needed to be the husband and father my family deserved.

Finding mentors outside the family structure proved invaluable. Family means well, but they're too emotionally invested. I was fortunate to develop a relationship with an older entrepreneur who had built and sold several successful businesses. Our conversations weren't just about strategy and markets - they were about the toll of leadership, the challenges of maintaining relationships, and the struggle to stay centered when everything around you is in constant motion.

Through my journey, I've learned that there are questions we must ask ourselves regularly - questions that every entrepreneur, young or old, new in the first couple of months or forty years in business, must face:

- Are you taking care of your health personally?
- Are you taking care of your mind and your soul?
- When was the last time you felt truly relaxed, not just physically tired?
- Do you have a space or activity that's solely for mental decompression?
- Who do you talk to when the weight feels too heavy to bear alone?
- Are you noticing the small changes in your behavior that others might already be seeing?
- Have you found your version of my canoe - that place or activity where clarity replaces chaos?

Chapter 9: The Silent Shift - Turning Inward

I often think about that day in the Maine hospital now that I am older and share as an advisor/mentor, not just as a cautionary tale but as a pivot point in my understanding of what it means to be a successful entrepreneur. Success isn't just measured in revenue growth or market share - it's measured in your ability to sustain both your business and yourself over the long haul. There's no need to carry the weight of the world on your back when sometimes a simple conversation or asking for help relieves a tremendous burden.

One final military strategy I can leave you with for your journey of reflection is Continuous Training and Development. The Navy emphasizes ongoing training to maintain readiness. Similarly, businesses benefit from investing in continuous employee development to enhance skills and adapt to industry changes and perhaps even life changes. Ensure you can adopt this mindset as you encounter shifts in your journey.

This pivotal moment in Maine emerges as more than just a wake-up call - it becomes a lens through which every major business decision would be viewed. The transformation from an extroverted problem-solver to a more contemplative leader shaped not only my approach to new ventures but also how I evaluated opportunities, built teams, and ultimately defined success.

The lessons learned during those three days in the hospital and in the soul-searching that followed became foundational to my entrepreneurial journey. They would influence crucial decisions about scaling businesses, entering new markets, and even knowing when to step back or step away. Sometimes, the most profound business lessons come not from success but from those moments when we're forced to stop and truly listen - to our bodies, to our minds, and to those who care enough to tell us when we're losing our way.

The challenges ahead - from building and selling companies to navigating economic uncertainties and managing rapid growth - would test these lessons repeatedly. Yet, having faced this moment of truth, I approached each new challenge with a different perspective, one that balanced ambition with

Depth and dividends

awareness and drive with discretion. It might help you to, as part of your journey, consider your mortality, and so a succession plan toolkit such as what I have included in *Appendix I* could help you.

As you explore these remaining sections, you'll see how, through Dickson's eyes, we can apply this transformed approach in practical steps that will lead to better business decisions and a more sustainable and fulfilling entrepreneurial life.

Toolkit items you need at this stage (See Appendix I)

1. *Succession planning guide*

CHAPTER 10
ENSURING YOUR BUSINESS LASTS FOR 100+ YEARS

> **Quick quiz. What do these 3 have in common?**
> - The World's Oldest Hotel. The world's oldest hotel is Japan's *Nishiyama Onsen Keiunkan*, and it has been in the same family for 52 generations, roughly 1,300 years, with each generation being about 25 years.
> - *McDonald* which is really the "largest small business in the world."
> - The *Coca-Cola* company, which was founded with the secret formulae of John Pemberton, the Alchemist of *Atlanta, Georgia* (1831-1888)).

The wrong answer is this: You can order a burger, fries, and a Coke from McDonald's and then have them delivered to your hotel room at *Nishiyama* after drifting through Tokyo.

The correct answer is a rather boring one. All these 3 businesses have outlived or outlasted the founders, and the reason for that is a simple word: "Internal controls." So, we are back to where I began my career - Internal controls, as I narrated to you in the introduction.

I will eventually share with you what I showed the son-in-law of the Ugandan president and what made him hire me. But before I do, what is the connection between internal controls and Terry's last story? He said:

Depth and dividends

> *"I had been so focused on maintaining the outward appearance of the confident, energetic business leader that I'd completely lost touch with my inner balance."*

You likely realize that Terry, in that last chapter, could have had a heart attack and died just like that!

It means that despite all the effort we put into our business, we are, after all, not immortal. That said and done, if you want to build a business that outlasts you and one that you can leave as a legacy to your children and children's children as some of the most successful businesses have done, then this requires the work of putting in place internal controls – and that's why for every Terry, there is a wingman in the background, helping to put in place the systems and controls to help run things efficiently, even when the Terrys of this world are carried off by their seafaring legs to the next venture.

What, then, are internal controls?

If the corporate governance I touched upon earlier is "the process by which the company's management is being monitored by someone else," then corporate governance sets the framework or the foundation for internal controls. Internal controls are, therefore, the detailed systems of checks and balances, including staff and management, to ensure that the entity continues to run smoothly – year in, year out, even as leadership changes.

Internal controls are things like counting inventory/stock every month to ensure that it is correct and accurate and checking independently that the store clerk has been doing the right thing.

You should note that the internal controls system that is put in place depends on the size and complexity of the organization. Some of the larger clients I dealt with, for example, had whole internal audit departments with several staff who looked at the company's control environment. Others were simple chicken farmers with just one key control: a hidden camera to catch those stealing eggs, especially if those on the camera footage did not look like the fantastic Mr. Fox.

Chapter 10: Ensuring Your Business Lasts For 100+ Years

The most sophisticated clients have software that can automatically detect anomalies.

A sound internal control system at its most basic, however, covers the following typical business cycles or processes:

- **Corporate governance** – Is a board running the company efficiently?
- **Sales and debtors** – can sales be unrecorded and debtors remain uncollected for long?
- **Purchases and creditors** – Can purchases be inflated and creditors not paid?

- **Fixed assets** – is there a fixed asset register to track assets?
- **Cash and Bank (or Treasury)** – Can cash be taken from the bank account without authorization?
- **Payroll** - Can payments be made to unauthorized staff?
- **IT and Insurance Risks** - are all assets adequately protected or insured?

I am sure you can see how much fun the above areas are! Anyway, all joking aside, for a growing company, this stuff is serious, and no matter how boring it is, you need to be aware of it. If you do not like it, outsource these internal control checks.

If you are interested or want to know what I shared with that famous son-in-law, I have attached a sample internal control program I originally used in Appendix II. The concepts I shared there made him pay me my first check, so you are stepping onto hallowed ground. I have since tweaked the checklist from my years of experience, so go on and see for yourself what makes accountants (or auditors) hot and excited!

In all seriousness, though, I strongly urge you to review the program in *Appendix II*. Use it as a checklist to see if your business meets these minimum requirements; if it doesn't, then you will probably be in much trouble and might need to call on Batman and Robin.

How internal controls ensure quality

Besides helping a company survive, one other reason internal control processes are critical for business success is for the simple reason that they ensure or help a business maintain quality. Quality brings in repeat customers or MONEY! But how do you define quality?

One of the best business books I have read is Michael Gerber's best-seller, The *E- Myth Revisited: Why Most Small Businesses Don't Work and What To Do About It*. He says that the fast-food chain McDonald's is a small business. He went on to explain that *McDonalds* is really the "largest small business in

Chapter 10: Ensuring Your Business Lasts For 100+ Years

the world." What he meant is that, in essence, every *McDonalds* is run by different business owners ("franchisees").

In the book, he describes why *McDonalds* is successful. One of the reasons is that its founder, Ray Kroc, set out to solve the franchise problem by thinking of how a small business could be run "by the lowest possible capable person."

This he did by having a detailed system of processes and procedures. These processes and procedures are so prescriptive that even the least educated or experienced person (no offense to McDonald's employees) can run it simply by following the instructions.

The logic applies to any other typical small (or big) business.

If you put in place internal control systems, including policies and procedures for what you do, then you can consistently produce a good/service at the same level of quality (whichever way you and your industry define or understand quality), and this can be done by the "lowest possible capable person."

It does not mean anyone can wake up today and go to the hospital to treat patients. Still, it means that in that business, the least capable can do the job required (for example, a junior doctor following instructions to diagnose patients like Mr. Ingram correctly).

As I already mentioned, the business can even (and should) run without you.

Every successful company has internal controls, policies, and procedures that are applied and followed (in many cases with military precision). This consistency is the solution to ensuring consistency and, hence, quality as perceived by the customer.

You have likely heard of the term Standard Operating Procedures (SOPs). This term originates from the Military. As Terry will tell you, the Navy relies on SOPs to maintain consistency and compliance. Businesses likewise can and should implement SOPs to ensure adherence to regulations and streamline operations; this is where controls come into play.

Depth and dividends

Quality, as a term, is quite intangible and cannot be easily described. Nevertheless, the logic is that if you have repeat customers, they are presumably returning because they are satisfied with your product/services. This means they are likewise satisfied inherently with the quality of your product/service.

Logically, it follows that if you consistently deliver your product/service at the same "level" and keep your customers returning, then you are offering a quality product!

The solution, therefore, to ensuring quality is to deliver a consistent product/service that meets your customers' needs every time -using internal control systems, and *McDonalds* does that well!

If you think about it, for their core customers, *Mcdonald's* offers a quality product because every time you go to *Mcdonald's*, the *Big Mac* burger tastes the same as the last time you went there, whether at 9.00 am or 9. pm, whether it was 5 years ago, or just the night before. It tastes the same whether you go to Paris and order *Le Big Mac* or travel to Amsterdam and order it with fries and an extra quarter pounder.

That is quality because (and this is critical) for a McDonalds customer, they meet that customer's needs - in the same way, every time.

To ensure quality, the solution, therefore, is to put in place policies and procedures (which is what controls are) to guide your staff in delivering the exact same product/service as they did yesterday, last year, etc. (you get the point).

The easiest means of ensuring quality control is through the segregation of duties. This means having someone independently check your work, your products, etc. You will be surprised at how many mistakes or errors can be picked up by this second review process.

If you don't have internal capacity, enter a contract or arrangement where you outsource this to an experienced reviewer and pay them a retainer or a

Chapter 10: Ensuring Your Business Lasts For 100+ Years

per-piece rate. If it is a part-time or fractional role, the extra money and a chance to use their expertise will benefit all.

A unique business environment case study: the United States

When implementing internal controls, it is critical to bear in mind the country within which the business operates. This covers the federal, state, and local levels for the US. How does an entrepreneur know where to look to understand the US business environment? Well, that is what a nerdy CPA is for!

So, until 2021, the *World Bank Group* published an annual report on the ease of doing business for countries worldwide. Since then, this has been replaced by Business Ready (B-Ready).

At the time of this book's publication, the most recent report on the U.S. was not yet ready, so the doing business report is the most relevant. That report ranked the US 6th globally out of 190 economies for ease of doing business.

The graph below shows that the US ranks well in some categories but not so well in others.

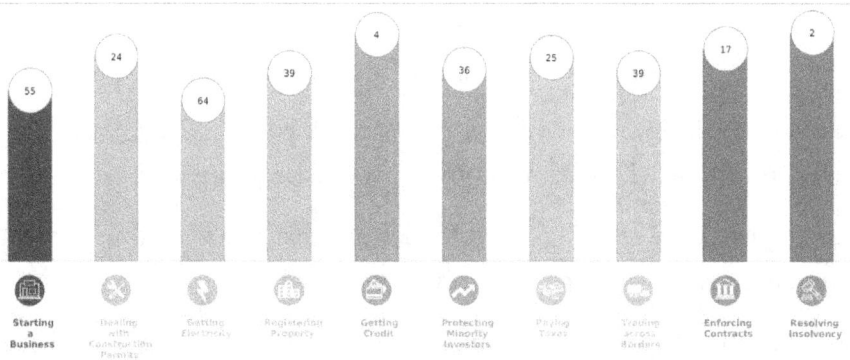

Source: *https://archive.doingbusiness.org/content/dam/doingBusiness/country/u/united-states/USA.pdf*

Depth and dividends

Based on the above graph, while we do well in areas such as resolving insolvency (#2) and getting credit (#4), we do not do so well compared to our overall 6th out of 190 nations ranking in the following areas:

- Getting electricity (64th)
- Starting a business (55th)
- Registering property (39th)
- Trading across borders (39th)
- Protecting minority investors (36th)

This means that when starting a business, you should be aware that the US can be complex compared to other countries. Additionally, if you are trading across borders, then you have double the complexity.

To aid you, I include in *Appendix III* a legal checklist to guide you on some things to consider as you start out in business. The checklist there helps you consider matters such as:

- Options for the right business structure (e.g., LLC, C-Corp, or S-Corp)
- Registering your business (federal, state, and local)
- Protecting intellectual property
- Drafting key business contracts
- Complying with tax regulations
- Tools and resources (e.g., *SBA, Legal Zoom, or Rocket Lawyer*)

Additionally, in Appendix IV, I provide a checklist for when you will import or export into the US for those doing cross-border business.

Have you enjoyed learning about the lessons that will keep your name and your family's name in business for 100+ years?

Well, our journey together is coming to an end, so now, we should review all the various lessons together. The next chapter is where the train journey ends, so come along with us for a final time.

Chapter 10: Ensuring Your Business Lasts For 100+ Years

Toolkit items you need at this stage.

1. *Compliance checklist (See Appendix I)*
2. *Sample internal control program (see Appendix II)*
3. *Legal Checklist for an Entrepreneur in the US (Appendix III)*
4. *Import and Export Checklist for an entrepreneur in the US (Appendix IV)*
5. *Common FAQs that US entrepreneurs ask (Appendix V)*

HOW THE STORY ENDS

When a U.S. Navy Submariner turned CEO and an ex-audit partner CPA walk into a room, it might sound like the beginning of a joke. Instead, it became the catalyst for transforming countless entrepreneurial dreams into reality.

This book, "Depth and Dividends," emerged from an unlikely alliance between a former submariner who rose to become a serial entrepreneur to CEO and a meticulous financial auditor - two different minds united by an unwavering belief that anyone with determination and the proper guidance can achieve extraordinary success.

The Power of Unexpected Partnerships

Great achievements rarely come from walking familiar paths. Our partnership proves that magic happens when you dare to combine seemingly different worlds:

- The disciplined precision of naval service with the exactitude of financial auditing.
- The bold vision of entrepreneurship with the careful stewardship of wealth.
- The depth of operational experience with the breadth of financial insight.

What makes this combination so powerful isn't just our different backgrounds - it's our shared passion for empowering others to reach heights they never thought possible. Every challenge we've faced, every obstacle we've overcome, has become a stepping stone for those who follow.

Why This Book Matters

"Depth and Dividends" isn't just another business book - it's your personal blueprint for success. Our message resonates because it's built on these eternal truths:

- Every challenge you face has been overcome by someone before you.
- Success leaves clues - you just need to know where to look.
- Your background doesn't limit your potential - it enhances it.
- Reaching out for help isn't a sign of weakness - it's a strategy for growth.
- The future belongs to those brave enough to shape it.

Your dreams aren't too big - they're just the beginning of what's possible.

A Final Analysis: Your Roadmap to Success

As Dickson would say (and I've learned to treasure his analytical wisdom), let's transform our combined experience into your action plan for success. We've navigated through crucial questions that every entrepreneur faces, providing you with tested solutions that work in the real world:

Understanding Your Readiness

Just as every successful mission requires thorough preparation, your entrepreneurial journey demands honest self-assessment and determined preparation. We've shown you how to:

- Transform your existing skills into business advantages
- Build unshakeable confidence through proper preparation
- Create support systems that ensure your success
- Turn your unique experiences into market opportunities

Financial Navigation

Like maintaining precise depth control, financial management requires constant attention and adjustment. But with the right tools and mindset, you can master:

- Creating robust business budgets that drive growth
- Identifying and tracking metrics that matter
- Managing tax obligations while maximizing opportunities
- Understanding and leveraging different business structures

Leadership in Deep Waters

Authentic leadership isn't about having all the answers - it's about building and guiding teams that can overcome any challenge. We've shown you how to:

- Build and inspire high-performing teams
- Turn crises into opportunities for growth
- Balance authority with humility
- Create cultures that attract and retain top talent

Scaling for Success

Growth isn't just about getting bigger - it's about getting better. You've learned strategies for:

- Scaling smartly and sustainably
- Making funding decisions that preserve your vision
- Optimizing resources for maximum impact
- Expanding into new markets with confidence

Setting Your Own Course

As you prepare to write your own success story, remember:

- Complex challenges often have simple solutions when viewed from the proper perspective

- The best leaders know when to seek guidance
- Details matter, but so does the bigger picture
- Your ego is often your biggest obstacle
- Success is sweeter when shared
- Your potential is limitless when you combine preparation with persistence

The story doesn't end here. For continued guidance and support, visit us at www.ingramadvisorygroup.com. Whether you're diving into new ventures or navigating rough waters, remember every successful journey begins with a single step - or, in our case, a single dive.

The Journey Continues

This isn't an ending - it's your beginning. Every principle, strategy, and insight we've shared is a tool in your arsenal for building something extraordinary. Your journey to success starts now, and you're better equipped than you realize.

Your Time Is Now

The business world has never offered more opportunities than it does today. Technology, global connectivity, and evolving markets create possibilities that didn't exist even a few years ago. You hold in your hands not just a book but a key to unlocking your entrepreneurial potential.

Remember:

- Every business success story started with someone exactly like you
- Your unique perspective is your competitive advantage
- Today's challenges are tomorrow's success stories
- You now have a framework that's been battle-tested
- You're part of a community of achievers and innovators

Looking to the Horizon

While "Depth and Dividends" marks the completion of one journey, it's really just the beginning. Stay tuned for our upcoming series that will dive even deeper into:

- Advanced growth strategies for established businesses
- International expansion and cross-border opportunities
- Revolutionary approaches to wealth creation and preservation
- The next generation of entrepreneurial innovation

And much more to come...

A Final Word From Us Both

Terry's Perspective: From the depths of naval service to the heights of business success, I've learned that the most extraordinary adventures begin with daring to dream big while acting with precision. Your journey starts now, and the possibilities are limitless.

Dickson's Analysis: Numbers (and the meticulous analysis behind them) tell stories of what's possible, and I've never seen more potential for success than in today's business environment. The future belongs to those who dare to dream big while planning smart - and that's precisely what you're prepared to do – are you ready for the train ride?

Your Next Chapter Begins

In *Appendix V*, we have also addressed the Common FAQs entrepreneurs ask, and we show you how this book can help you address them, but as you close this book, know that you're not just prepared - you're poised for greatness. The strategies, insights, and wisdom shared here are your foundation. What you build on that foundation is limited only by your imagination and determination.

For continued guidance, support, and updates on our upcoming series, we really encourage you to visit us at www.ingramadvisorygroup.com. Remember: every great success story has a beginning, and yours is just getting started.

The horizon ahead is bright, the opportunities are boundless, and your journey to extraordinary success begins now. Welcome to your future - we can't wait to see what you'll achieve.

End.

BOOK II
APPENDICES &
SUPPLEMENTARY MATERIAL

APPENDIX I
SAMPLE BUSINESS TOOLKITS

1. Market Research Template

Use this to help you start putting together your ideas for a business

Category	Details
Target Audience	*Describe the primary customer demographic.*
Customer Needs	*List the specific needs of your product/service addresses.*
Competitor Analysis	*Outline main competitors, their strengths, and weaknesses.*
Unique Selling Point	*What sets your product/service apart?*
Pricing Strategy	*Pricing model and how it compares to competitors.*
Potential Challenges	*Risks in the market and how to address them.*

2. Startup Budget Template

Use this to help you think of items when putting together a budget for building the business.

Expense Category	Description	Estimated Cost ($)
Office Rent	*Monthly office space cost*	1,500
Equipment	*Computers, printers, etc.*	2,000

Expense Category	Description	Estimated Cost ($)
Marketing	*Campaigns, ads*	1,000
Legal Fees	*Incorporation, contracts*	800
Initial Inventory	*Product stock*	3,000
Miscellaneous	*Additional expenses*	500
Total		8,800

3. Cash Flow Tracker

Cash flows are highly critical for a business. The Profit and Loss account shows you how much you are making, but the cash flow shows you things not in the profit and loss category, such as payments you make to repay your debtors. A typical cash flow is categorized as follows:

- **Operating cash flows** – your day-to-day business activities like revenue, expenses, debtors, and creditors.
- **Investing cash flows.** These are items like the purchase of property, plant, and equipment and investments you make, such as stocks and bonds.
- **Financing cash flows.** This is for items like loans you borrow or additional capital you put into the business.

Month	Operating cash flows ($)	Investing Cash flows ($)	Financing Cash flows ($)	Net Cash Flow ($)
January	10,000	2,500	1,500	6,000
February	12,000	2,500	2,000	7,500
March	15,000	2,500	2,500	10,000

Appendix I: Sample Business TOOLKITS

4. Break-Even Analysis Worksheet

Many startups need to figure out how to price 1 unit or how to know how many units to sell so that they can cover the costs or start to make a profit (the break-even point). This summary helps you do that.

Metric	Value
Fixed Costs ($)	2,500
Variable Costs ($)	1,500 per unit
Selling Price ($)	5,000 per unit
Break-Even Point	Calculate the total units needed to cover costs.

5. Team Motivation Plan

Managing the team is extremely critical in business, but how do you keep them motivated? The template below can help you in developing that plan.

Goal	Action Steps	Timeline
Increase team morale	Monthly check-ins, team outings	Monthly
Recognize achievements	Employee of the Month program	Monthly
Improve communication	Weekly team meetings	Weekly

6. Crisis Response Framework (or war gaming)

In business, disaster can happen at any time, whichever way you define disaster, but if you plan, or what some businesses call "contingency planning" or "disaster recovery." In the Navy, the term used was war gaming. You simulate scenarios and then develop strategic responses to deal with them. The framework below can be expanded, but it gives you the idea.

Crisis Type	Immediate Steps/war game options/scenarios	Key Contact
Financial	Freeze spending, reassess budgets	CFO
Operational	Notify teams, reroute resources	Operations Manager
Reputational	Issue a statement, monitor media	PR Manager

7. Compliance Checklist

In business, there are different rules and regulations that you need to consider. You must consider, for example:

- *Regulatory environment – e.g., FDA, USDA, EPA, and other agency regulations for a US business.*
- *Customs and Border Protection (CBP) Procedures such as proper classification of goods under the Harmonized Tariff Schedule (HTS) for importing into the US.*
- *Tariffs and Duties: Understanding applicable tariffs and how to calculate them; navigating trade agreements and potential exemptions; dealing with changing trade policies and tariff structures.*

The framework below will help you understand the most critical laws and regulations. Including the complete list in your board meetings or management meetings as you build your team is good practice.

Regulation Type	Compliance Requirement	Status
Tax Compliance	Quarterly filing, tax payments	Up-to-date
Employment Law	Minimum wage, anti-discrimination	Up-to-date
Data Privacy	Secure customer data	Review in progress

8. Tax Planning Basics

Tax rules in different countries vary, and in places such as the US, they are incredibly complex. You likely need to work with your CPA regularly to ensure you are up to date. Nevertheless, as a business owner, it helps to know the "lay of the land" – what is the big picture of the critical areas of tax you need to be aware of to ensure that your team is doing the right thing? The framework below helps you put the correct reporting framework for your team to report to you.

Tax Category	Description	Action Plan
Income Tax	Estimated annual tax obligation	Schedule quarterly payments
Sales Tax	Collect and remit sales tax	Monthly filing
Payroll Tax	Employee withholdings	Automated payroll system

9. Risk Assessment Template

In doing business, it is critical for you to know the key risks your company is subject to and know the impact and the likelihood of the risk. Knowing this can help you develop a means of minimizing the risks, and in conjunction with your war gaming, you can reduce the number of crises that occur. The template below can be built up in conjunction with your team and/or your advisors.

Risk	Impact Level (1-5)	Likelihood (1-5)	Mitigation Strategy
Supply Chain Disruption	4	3	Diversify suppliers
Cash Flow Shortage	5	4	Secure line of credit
Market Competition	3	4	Focus on unique offerings

10. Scaling Readiness Checklist

The growth of business is good news for most entrepreneurs, but there is the risk of growing too fast and being unprepared. The checklist below is a tool you can use to assess how ready you are for growth.

Readiness Factor	Criteria	Status
Consistent Profitability	12+ months of profits	Yes
Demand for Product	Growing inquiries/orders	Yes
Operational Capacity	Ready to handle increased demand	No

11. Negotiation Prep Sheet

When negotiating in business or closing deals, it helps to have the right tools. The negotiation prep sheet tool below can help you close the deal by helping you assemble your negotiation strategy.

Objective	[Describe the primary goal]
Key Points to Address	*[List key issues/concerns]*
Concessions Allowed	*[List flexible points]*
Non-Negotiable Terms	*[List firm terms]*

12. Deal Comparison Matrix

When negotiating deals, the deal comparison matrix can help you compare your options and choose the best deal.

Option	Cost ($)	Benefits	Drawbacks
Option 1	5,000	Flexible terms	Higher cost
Option 2	3,500	Lower cost	Strict terms

13. Annual Business Review Template

To prepare your business for long-term success, it helps to have annual reviews of what has gone well or what needs improvement. The template below can be used as part of this review.

Category	Goal/Result	Status
Financial	Revenue, net profit targets	On track
Operational	Efficiency, cost control	Needs Improvement
Customer Satisfaction	Survey scores, repeat purchases	Excellent

14. Succession Planning Guide

Successful businesses are prepared for anything, including when a leader must be replaced due to death, incapacity, retirement, or a myriad of factors. Be ready for this using a succession planning guide.

Position	Successor Candidate(s)	Training Needs
CEO	Jane Doe, VP of Operations	Leadership training
CFO	John Smith, Controller	Advanced finance

15. Funding Decision Matrix

The Funding Decision Matrix helps entrepreneurs evaluate the best financing option for their business by comparing factors such as control, cost, and growth potential. The matrix categorizes funding options into self-funding, loans, investors, and grants and evaluates their advantages and challenges. Use the following matrix to evaluate your options:

Funding Option	Control (Retain/Share)	Cost (Interest/Equity)	Growth Potential	Challenges
Self-Funding	Retain Full Control	No Interest	Limited to Personal Resources	Risk of Depleting Savings
Loans	Retain Full Control	Interest Payments	Moderate	Requires Creditworthiness and Repayment
Investors	Share Control	Equity Given	High	Dilution of Ownership
Grants	Retain Full Control	No Cost	Moderate	Competitive and Time-Intensive Application

APPENDIX II
SAMPLE INTERNAL CONTROL PROGRAM

1 GOVERNANCE

Potential Risks:

- The Board of Directors (BOD) does not have procedures in place that allow it to fulfill all its responsibilities in managing the business and its finances
- The lack of clear direction results in weak governance and reduces accountability and effectiveness

Controlling the Risks:

- A Scheme of Delegation and Summary of Financial Delegation (For example, a signatory list) are in place, which charges the BOD with the responsibility of managing the business and its finances
- Up to date, agreed Terms of Reference exist for the BOD and its committees.
- For day-to-day operational matters, the BOD has determined how they will delegate matters to members of management and staff
- There is a clearly defined business organization structure, financial management policy, and finance procedure.

	CONTROL	STATE HOW THE BUSINESS MEETS THE CONTROL	CONTROL ADEQUATE Yes/No
1	The roles and responsibilities of the governing body and its committees have been set out in writing.		
2	The roles, responsibilities, and memberships are reviewed and amended as required.		
3	There is clear documentation regarding the delegation of staff members with financial responsibilities.		
4	The board reviews and agrees upon the documentation on an annual basis.		
5	All board members, management, and staff with financial responsibilities have access to and an understanding of the Business's Financial Policies and Procedures Manual.		
6	Governing Body and committee meetings allow decisions to be taken in line with the board's and others' deadlines.		
7	All decisions, who has made them, and what action must be taken are clearly documented and distributed to all concerned.		
8	An up-to-date record of "related party transactions" is maintained of business		

Appendix II: Sample internal control program

	interests for directors and staff who influence financial decisions.		
9	Procedures are in place to ensure that financial control is maintained in the absence of key personnel.		
10	Proper accounting records are maintained and retained in accordance with the document retention schedule.		
11	All accounting records are retained securely, and access is controlled.		
12	A policy has been made available to all staff to enable them to raise serious concerns regarding any aspect of the business's work.		

Based on the responses to the above, what is the:

Likelihood / Impact of the risk	H / M / L
Action required	Y / N

Key:

H- High

M- Medium

L- Low

2 FINANCIAL PLANNING AND BUDGETARY CONTROL

Potential Risks:

- Failure to plan over several years and target resources to specific priorities reduces effectiveness, levels of improvement, and potential for growth
- The business fails to manage within its available resources - at best, becoming overdrawn at the bank, and at worst, putting its going concern status at risk

Controlling the Risks:

- The Strategic Development Plan (SDP) will generally cover 3-5 years. To ensure that resources are available to meet its objectives, there must be clear links from the SDP to the business's annual budget
- Budgeting and subsequent regular budget monitoring are essential to sound financial management.

	CONTROL	STATE HOW THE BUSINESS MEETS THE CONTROL	CONTROL ADEQUATE Yes/No
1	The financial resources required to meet the business's goals and strategic objectives are identified in the SDP.		
2	Sufficient detail exists in the SDP to provide the basis for constructing budget plans for the next and future financial years.		
3	Procedures are in place to allow the board and staff adequate time to appraise the likely costs and benefits of any new initiative.		
4	Actual and projected customer numbers are closely monitored.		

5	Historic spending patterns are not unhelpfully perpetuated when constructing the budget.		
6	The Board receives regular, informative, understandable, and budget monitoring reports that include commitments, outturn forecasts, and variations.		
7	Bank reconciliation takes place promptly.		

Based on the responses to the above, what is the:

Likelihood / Impact of the risk	H / M / L
Action required	Y / N

4 PURCHASING

Potential Risks:

- The business does not achieve the Best Value
- Suppliers are not chosen impartially or based on fair competition, leading to a potential for fraud or damage to reputation
- Lack of commitments can result in overspending
- Quotations/tenders are not sought in line with the business's policy
- Spending via credit /debit cards is not in accordance with the procedures agreed by the board

Controlling the Risks:

- Evidence to show that the business has obtained Best Value for its purchases should be retained
- Commitments, except for utilities, should be placed on the business's finance system PRIOR to the order being sent.
- Sufficient quotations and tenders should be sought in accordance with the business's regulations before any decision to purchase is made.
- The board should be involved in decisions.

Depth and dividends

	CONTROL	STATE HOW THE BUSINESS MEETS THE CONTROL	CONTROL ADEQUATE Yes/No
1	Price, quality, and fitness for purpose are considered when purchasing goods or services.		
2	Sufficient tenders and quotations are obtained.		
3	Board approval is obtained for all expenditures in line with authority limits.		
4	Service contracts are delivered in accordance with the contract specification.		
5	Except for utilities, an official pre-numbered order is generated for the purchase of goods and services (including verbal, electronic, or faxed emergency purchases).		
6	Controls are in place over reimbursement of staff purchases (where personal checks or credit cards have been used)		
7	Orders are used only for goods and services provided to the business and not for private use by staff.		
8	All orders and deliveries are authorized/checked with adequate segregation of duties.		
9	Outstanding/late orders are monitored regularly.		

10	Procedures surrounding the use of credit/debit cards are being followed, and controls are being implemented.		

Based on the responses to the above, what is the:

Likelihood / Impact of the risk	H / M / L
Action required	Y / N

5. PAYMENT OF INVOICES

Potential Risks:

- Payments are made for goods or services which have not been received or ordered by the business
- Payments are made for the wrong amount
- Payments are made to the wrong supplier
- Payments are duplicated
- Interest charges are incurred due to late payment of invoices

Controlling the Risks:

- There is adequate segregation of duties. No one person should be able to order, receive, and pay for goods and services
- Before any payment is made, there are appropriate checks to ensure the accuracy of the invoice, that it agrees with the order, and that the goods or services have been received.
- The person authorizing payment of the invoice is sure it relates to business expenditure and has been checked for accuracy.

Depth and dividends

	CONTROL	STATE HOW THE BUSINESS MEETS THE CONTROL	CONTROL ADEQUATE Yes/No
1	Procedures are in place to ensure that what has been delivered is what was initially ordered.		
2	More than one person authorizes the order and certifies the invoice.		
3	Only original invoices are processed for payment once checked, coded, and certified.		
4	Procedures are in place and followed regarding the processing of electronic invoices.		
5	Invoices are certified for payment in accordance with the delegation of authority scheme.		
6	All paid invoices are marked in some way to prevent duplicate processing.		
7	All invoices are paid in accordance with the agreed payment terms.		
8	Items are recorded on the inventory if appropriate.		
9	Check runs are reviewed prior to the check being signed.		
10	Checks are not pre-signed		

| 11 | Tax (e.g., Sales Tax/VAT) is accurately calculated and correctly applied. | | |

Based on the responses to the above, what is the:

Likelihood / Impact of the risk	H / M / L
Action required	Y / N

6. PETTY CASH

Potential Risks:

- Petty cash is used to bypass routine payment procedures
- Duplicate payments are made through the creditor or payroll systems
- Personal checks are cashed from the petty cash float
- Cash float is held in an insecure place
- Reimbursement is made without appropriate paperwork
- Cash is handed out in advance of purchase without receipt
- Income & expenditure is not recorded promptly
- The total of cash in hand and receipts do not match the agreed limit

Controlling the Risks:

- Petty cash is only available in emergencies or for small-value items that would be inappropriate to put through creditors or payroll systems.
- The board/management should agree on the procedures and a limit above which petty cash cannot be used
- Although relatively small amounts are involved in the transactions, the same accounting principles apply, i.e., no one person should be responsible for authorizing, paying out, and reconciling the petty cash
- The petty cash should be reconciled at least monthly
- Any discrepancies should be reported immediately
- The petty cash should always be reimbursed back to the agreed limit

Depth and dividends

	CONTROL	STATE HOW THE BUSINESS MEETS THE CONTROL	CONTROL ADEQUATE Yes/No
1	There are written procedures for the administration and use of the petty cash.		
2	The level of the petty cash float held is appropriate to the needs of the business and has been agreed upon by the board/management.		
3	The cash float is held securely, and access is limited to authorized staff.		
4	Payments from petty cash are limited to minor expenditure items.		
5	All expenditure is supported by a receipt (VAT where possible), is signed for by the recipient, countersigned by an authorized member of staff, and presented in a timely manner.		
6	The petty cash is reconciled regularly, at least monthly.		
7	Claims for reimbursement of the imprest account are made regularly and are authorized by staff with delegated responsibility.		

8	An independent reconciliation of the imprest account is undertaken regularly (at least six months) by someone other than the account administrator.		
9	Personal checks are not cashed from the cash float.		

Based on the responses to the above, what is the:

Likelihood / Impact of the risk	H / M / L
Action required	Y / N

7 INCOME

Potential Risks:

- Charges or rates for goods/services are not appropriate and/or consistently applied
- Income is not banked promptly
- Insurance limits for holding cash are exceeded
- Cash and checks are not held securely
- Inadequate procedures for the collection and recording of income
- Income is not recorded/goes astray
- Controlling the Risks:
- Charging policies for goods/services or standard price lists are established, agreed upon, and reviewed by the board on an annual basis
- Official, pre-numbered receipts or other formal documentation should be kept for all income received
- Procedures exist and are followed for the collection and banking of income

Depth and dividends

	CONTROL	STATE HOW THE BUSINESS MEETS THE CONTROL	CONTROL ADEQUATE Yes/No
1	The charging policies above are up to date and set out details of charges, discounts, and concessions. They are reviewed regularly.		
2	There are procedures for reviewing and monitoring all income due to the business.		
3	Invoices are sent as soon as a debt arises.		
4	The business requests that all checks be made payable to the business.		
5	All staff are aware of the procedures in business for collecting money and handing it over to the person responsible for banking.		
6	All income received is recorded and receipted where applicable in accordance with the agreed segregation of duties.		
7	All machines that take money, including telephones, are emptied regularly, and two people count the cash.		
8	All cash and receipt books are held securely in a safe or fireproof, lockable receptacle.		
9	Access to the safe is restricted to authorized staff.		
10	Banking is not less than weekly, ensuring that cash is within the insurance limits.		

Appendix II: Sample internal control program

11	Income received is not used to encash personal checks or other payments.		
12	Income is banked promptly and intact.		
13	There is an independent monthly reconciliation of the income received and the income banked.		
14	There is proof of monies collected by a security company.		

Based on the responses to the above, what is the:

Likelihood / Impact of the risk	H / M / L
Action required	Y / N

8 FIXED ASSETS

Potential Risks:

- No independent record of fixed assets held within the business
- Losses are not identified if the asset register is not reviewed and updated regularly
- Lack of control over stocks of materials and other consumables results in loss and waste, as well as stock being unavailable when needed.
- Items are lost or mislaid, possibly damaged or stolen without recognition until they are required and cannot be used or cannot be found
- Lack of security marking reduces the chance of recovery in the event of theft.
- Lost/stolen items cannot be identified/recovered
- There is no plan for the use, maintenance, and development of the business building(s)

Depth and dividends

Controlling the Risks:

- A designated staff member is responsible for the fixed asset inventory system. This person ensures that the register/inventory is up to date
- An annual check of the inventory is carried out by someone other than the person who maintains the register
- Items 'loaned' to staff are recorded
- Items taken off-site are logged out and signed back in again
- Items should be security marked with an asset number or other identifying information
- The business's maintenance plan should work in conjunction with the annual budget and Strategic Development Plan (SDP)

	CONTROL	STATE HOW THE BUSINESS MEETS THE CONTROL	CONTROL ADEQUATE Yes/No
1	An up-to-date inventory of all assets above the level agreed by the board and those deemed portable/desirable is maintained.		
2	An independent officer undertakes an annual check to ensure the physical items agree to those listed on the inventory. The inventory is signed and dated to confirm agreement.		
3	All discrepancies are investigated, and any over a specific value are reported to the board.		
4	All property taken off the business site is recorded and signed for, and its return is recorded.		
5	All write-offs and the disposal of surplus stocks and equipment are undertaken in accordance with written policies/Financial Regulations and recorded as such.		

6	There is a procedure for the security of premises; it is adequate and reviewed regularly.		
7	The number of keys to buildings, safes, etc., is limited to the minimum practical, and access to them is controlled.		
8	All keys to safes, cash boxes, and other receptacles in which money or valuables are secured are always carried on the person of those responsible.		

Based on the responses to the above, what is the:

Likelihood / Impact of the risk	H / M / L
Action required	Y / N

9 DATA SECURITY

Potential Risks:

- The business does not have an appropriate IT and data protection policy
- Insufficient or irregular password security and access levels
- System is insecure, and/or individuals have inappropriate access rights
- Inability to recover lost data
- Lack of up-to-date data protection software
- Unlicensed software is used

Controlling the Risks:

- Set up an IT and data protection policy
- Access to software is adequately restricted and protected
- Regular back-ups are taken, including an off-site copy
- Regular updating of the virus protection
- A Policy regarding the use of computers is in place

Depth and dividends

	CONTROL	STATE HOW THE BUSINESS MEETS THE CONTROL	CONTROL ADEQUATE Yes/No
1	Access to computers and data is limited, and passwords are changed regularly.		
2	Personal information held is in line with the Business's Data Protection policy.		
3	A designated officer has been identified to manage the IT environment.		
4	Regular backups are taken to allow the rebuilding of systems. One complete backup is held off-site to safeguard against the loss of data.		
5	Users are aware of the need to protect the computer system against viruses by not using their software.		
6	The system is adequately protected against viruses.		
7	All software applications are licensed.		
8	Staff are aware of the accepted use of the IT equipment.		
9	The system is kept up to date and accurate, e.g., new starters are given access rights where appropriate, and leavers' rights are removed in a timely manner.		

Appendix II: Sample internal control program

Based on the responses to the above, what is the:

Likelihood / Impact of the risk	H / M / L
Action required	Y / N

10 INSURANCE/RISK

Potential Risks:

- Risk Assessments are not conducted regularly, inc. Health & Safety checks
- Sums insured are inadequate
- Additional items are not added to policies promptly
- Losses are not reported

Controlling the Risks:

- Risks should be reviewed on an annual basis
- Alterations to policies should be notified to the Insurer

	CONTROL	STATE HOW THE BUSINESS MEETS THE CONTROL	CONTROL ADEQUATE Yes/No
1	There is a methodology for identifying, assessing, and addressing risks and documenting the process.		
2	All risks are reviewed annually to ensure that the sums insured are commensurate with the risks.		
3	There is a procedure for notifying the insurer immediately of all new risks, property, equipment, and vehicles that require insurance or where it affects existing insurance.		

4	The business immediately notifies insurers of all accidents, losses, or incidents that may give rise to an insurance claim.		
5	Regular Health & Safety checks are carried out, with reports being forwarded to the board.		

Based on the responses to the above, what is the:

Likelihood / Impact of the risk	H / M / L
Action required	Y / N

Checklist Completed by: ....

Date:...............

Reviewed by: -...................................

Date: ....

APPENDIX III
LEGAL CHECKLIST FOR STARTING A BUSINESS

The checklist below uses a US environment as a reference; you can tailor it accordingly with your specific jurisdiction in mind.

1. Choose the Right Business Structure

Options:

- Sole Proprietorship
- Partnership (General or Limited)
- Limited Liability Company (LLC)
- Corporation (C-Corp or S-Corp)

Action Steps:

- Research the pros and cons of each structure (e.g., liability protection, taxation).
- File the necessary formation documents with your state (e.g., Articles of Organization for LLCs or Articles of Incorporation for Corporations).

Tools/Resources:

- [SBA.gov] (https://www.sba.gov) for guidance.

- Legal platforms like [LegalZoom] (https://www.legalzoom.com) or [Rocket Lawyer] (https://www.rocketlawyer.com).

2. Register Your Business

Federal Registration:

- Obtain an Employer Identification Number (EIN) from the IRS for tax purposes.

Resource: [IRS EIN Application] (https://www.irs.gov/businesses/small-businesses-self-employed/apply-for-an-employer-identification-number-ein-online).

State Registration:

- Register your business name with your state's Secretary of State.
- File a Doing Business As (DBA) if operating under a trade name.

Local Registration:

- Check city/county requirements for business licenses or permits.

3. Protect Intellectual Property

Trademarks:

- Register your business name, logo, and tagline with the U.S. Patent and Trademark Office (USPTO).
- Resource: [USPTO.gov] (https://www.uspto.gov).

Copyrights:

- Protect original content like blogs, videos, or designs.

Patents:

- If you have an innovative product or process, consider applying for a patent.

4. Draft Key Business Contracts

Common Contracts:

- Operating Agreement (LLC) or Corporate Bylaws (Corporation).
- Employment and Independent Contractor Agreements.
- Non-Disclosure Agreements (NDAs) for sensitive information.
- Partnership Agreements if applicable.
- Service or Sales Contracts with clients/customers.

Tools:

- Contract templates from [Rocket Lawyer] (https://www.rocketlawyer.com).
- Seek legal advice for customization.

5. Comply with Tax Regulations

Federal Taxes:

- Understand your business's tax obligations (e.g., income tax, self-employment tax).
- File taxes annually (quarterly if required).
- Resource: [IRS Small Business Taxes]
- (https://www.irs.gov/businesses/small-businesses-self-employed).

State and Local Taxes:

- Register for state-specific taxes, such as sales tax or franchise tax.
- Check city/county tax obligations.

Tools:

- Accounting software like QuickBooks or Xero.
- Consult with a CPA.

6. Obtain Necessary Permits and Licenses

Industry-Specific Permits:

- E.g., health permits for restaurants and real estate licenses for brokers.

Zoning Permits:

- Check zoning laws if operating from a physical location.

Tools:

- Use the [SBA's License and Permit Tool] (https://www.sba.gov/starting-business/business-licenses-permits) to identify requirements.

7. Set Up Proper Employment Practices

Hire Legally:

- Verify employees' work eligibility with Form I-9 (via [E-Verify] (https://www.e-verify.gov)).

Employment Laws:

- Comply with wage laws (e.g., minimum wage, overtime).
- Provide workers' compensation insurance if required.

Employee Handbook:

- Draft policies on conduct, benefits, and grievance procedures.

8. Ensure Compliance with Data Privacy Laws

If Collecting Personal Data:

- Follow laws like GDPR (if international) or CCPA (California Consumer Privacy Act).
- Use secure systems to store data and draft a Privacy Policy.

Tools:

- Online legal tools like [Termly] (https://termly.io) for creating Privacy Policies.

9. Protect Against Liability

Business Insurance:

- General Liability Insurance.
- Professional Liability Insurance (for service providers).
- Product Liability Insurance (if applicable).

Workers' Compensation Insurance:

- Required for most employers.

10. Create a Disaster Recovery Plan

- Include contingency plans for legal, financial, or operational crises.
- Document procedures for cybersecurity incidents or natural disasters.

11. Stay Updated with Regulatory Changes

Federal:

- Monitor IRS updates, labor laws, and industry-specific changes.

State/Local:

- Sign up for notifications from state and local agencies.

12. Tools and Resources for Entrepreneurs

Legal Platforms:

- [LegalZoom] (https://www.legalzoom.com)
- [Nolo] (https://www.nolo.com)
- [Rocket Lawyer] (https://www.rocketlawyer.com)

Accounting and Tax Software:

- QuickBooks, Xero, TurboTax.

Government Resources:

- [SBA.gov] (https://www.sba.gov)
- [IRS.gov] (https://www.irs.gov)
- [USPTO.gov] (https://www.uspto.gov)

APPENDIX IV
IMPORT/EXPORT CHECKLIST FOR US ENTREPRENEURS

1. Determine Product Eligibility

Understand Your Product:

- Classify your goods using the Harmonized Tariff Schedule (HTS).
- Verify whether your goods are restricted, prohibited, or require special permits.

Tools/Resources:

- [HTS Online Lookup] (https://hts.usitc.gov)
- Contact the U.S. Customs and Border Protection (CBP) for guidance.

2. Register Your Business

Federal Requirements:

- Obtain an Employer Identification Number (EIN) from the IRS.
- Apply for an Import-Export License, if required (most products do not need one, but some restricted items do).

Resources:

- [CBP Licensing Guide] (https://www.cbp.gov)

3. Understand Import/Export Compliance

Import Compliance:

- File an Importer Security Filing (ISF) for ocean shipments.
- Ensure compliance with Federal Trade Commission (FTC) labeling requirements (e.g., "Made in [Country]").
- Pay applicable duties and tariffs.

Export Compliance:

- Verify if your product is controlled under the Export Administration Regulations (EAR).
- Check destination country restrictions through the Bureau of Industry and Security (BIS).

Tools/Resources:

- [Export.gov Compliance Guide] (https://www.export.gov)

4. Obtain Required Permits

Import Permits:

- For restricted items like alcohol, firearms, or certain foods, obtain permits from relevant agencies (e.g., Alcohol and Tobacco Tax and Trade Bureau (TTB)).

Export Licenses:

- For controlled goods, apply for an export license via the Simplified Network Application Process Redesign (SNAP-R) system.

Resources:

- [BIS SNAP R] (https://www.bis.doc.gov/index.php/licensing/simplified-network-application-process-redesign-snap-r)

5. Register with Customs

Obtain a Customs Bond:

- Required for importing goods valued over $2,500 or regulated items.
- Use the Automated Commercial Environment (ACE) portal to manage customs filings.

Resources:

- [ACE Portal] (https://www.cbp.gov/trade/automated)

6. Verify Trade Agreements and Tariffs

- Check if your product qualifies for reduced tariffs or duty-free status under trade agreements (e.g., USMCA, Generalized System of Preferences (GSP)).

Resources:

- [Trade Agreements Guide] (https://ustr.gov)

7. Understand Shipping Requirements

- Select the appropriate Incoterms (International Commercial Terms) for your transactions.
- Ensure that shipping labels, bills of lading, and commercial invoices meet international standards.

Resources:

- [International Chamber of Commerce: Incoterms] (https://iccwbo.org/resources-for-business/incoterms-rules/)

8. Pay Duties and Taxes

- Calculate customs duties using the HTS classification.
- Ensure payment of state-specific taxes, such as excise taxes, if applicable.

Resources:

- Use the CBP Duty Calculator.

9. Ensure Proper Documentation

Import Documents:

- Purchase Order.
- Commercial Invoice.
- Packing List.
- Bill of Lading or Airway Bill.
- Customs Entry Form (e.g., CBP Form 3461).

Export Documents:

- Commercial Invoice.
- Packing List.
- Certificate of Origin.
- Shipper's Export Declaration (SED), filed through the Automated Export System (AES).

Tools:

- [AESDirect Filing Portal] (https://www.cbp.gov/trade/aes/aestir/filing-exports-aes)

10. Stay Updated on Trade Regulations

- Monitor updates on tariffs, quotas, and sanctions.
- Subscribe to newsletters from CBP, BIS, or other relevant agencies.

Resources:

- [CBP Trade Updates] (https://www.cbp.gov/trade)
- [BIS Regulations] (https://www.bis.doc.gov)

11. Partner with Experts

Customs Broker:

- Helps ensure compliance and manage documentation.

Freight Forwarder:

- Manages logistics, shipping, and international regulations.

Resources:

- [National Customs Brokers & Forwarders Association of America (NCBFAA)] (https://www.ncbfaa.org)

12. Protect Your Business

Insurance:

- Purchase cargo insurance to cover losses or damage during transit.

Risk Mitigation:

- Conduct due diligence on trading partners.
- Use Letters of Credit (LC) for secure payment terms.

APPENDIX V
COMMON FAQS THAT ENTREPRENEURS ASK

When starting and structuring a Business

Q: How do I determine if I am ready to start a business?

A: Ask yourself:

- Do you have a clear mission or purpose for the business?
- Are your finances stable enough to cover at least 6–12 months of expenses?
- Have you researched the market to validate your idea?

Start with tools like the Market Research Template in *Appendix I* to evaluate your target audience, competitors, and potential challenges. Additionally, the journey Terry covers in *Chapter 7, Navigating the Seas to Entrepreneurship*, will help you.

Q: What is the best way to find a business idea that aligns with my skills?

A: Leverage your background and strengths. For example:

- Military veterans might consider industries like logistics, leadership consulting, or cybersecurity.
- Financial professionals might focus on financial planning or tax consultancy.

Use a SWOT Analysis Framework (Strengths, Weaknesses, Opportunities, Threats) to match your skills with market gaps, or consider using psychometric tools such as

Gallup's *StrengthsFinder* to know yourself and pivot to areas where your strengths will best be used.

Q: What are the first legal and financial steps to take when starting a business (for example, in the U.S.)?

A: Follow these critical 1st steps:

- Choose a business structure (LLC, sole proprietorship, corporation).
- Register your business and obtain an Employer Identification Number (EIN).
- Set up a business bank account and accounting system.
- Research and acquire any necessary licenses or permits for your industry.

Use the Startup Budget Template (*Appendix I*) to organize costs. See *Appendix III and IV* for the legal checklist and Import/Export Checklist, respectively, when considering the various areas in the US.

Managing Finances

Q: How do I create a business budget?

A: A budget outlines your expected revenue and expenses. Start with:

- Fixed costs: Rent, insurance, and salaries.
- Variable costs: Inventory and utilities.
- Emergency reserves: At least 3-6 months of operating costs.

Use the Cash Flow Tracker Template (*Appendix I*) to monthly monitor your inflow and outflow.

Q: What are the most important financial metrics to monitor?

A: Key Performance Indicators (KPIs) include:

- Net Profit Margin: Revenue after deducting all expenses.
- Cash Flow: The difference between incoming and outgoing cash.
- Customer Acquisition Cost (CAC): The cost of gaining a new customer.
- Break-Even Point: The revenue needed to cover expenses.

Work with your CPA to build the KPIs critical for your industry sector in addition to these core ones.

Q: How do I manage taxes and avoid penalties?

A: Implement these practices:

- Track deductible expenses (office supplies, mileage, etc.).
- Use accounting software like QuickBooks to keep records accurate.
- Pay quarterly estimated taxes to avoid penalties.

Speak to a CPA who specializes in tax to help you identify the critical tax credits and deductions available for your business and sector.

Leadership and Management

Q: How do I build a strong team with limited resources?

A: Focus on:

- Cultural Fit: Hire people who align with your company's mission.
- Skill Development: Invest in low-cost training programs.
- Recognition: Non-monetary rewards like "Employee of the Month" can boost morale.

Use the *Team Motivation Plan* in *Appendix I* and check out *Chapter 6: Why Businesses Fail for the special section on high-performing* teams.

Q: How do I handle a crisis in my business?

A: Use the Crisis Response Framework (*Appendix I*):

- Identify the type of crisis (financial, operational, reputational).
- Take immediate action: Freeze non-essential spending in financial crises or issue a public statement in reputational crises.
- Have a Crisis Response Team with critical contacts for each type of crisis.

Scaling and Growth

Q: What are the best ways to scale a small business?

A: Start with these strategies:

- Optimize operations before expansion.
- Expand products/services into related markets.
- Invest in digital marketing and e-commerce (See *Chapter 4: Secrets millionaires use to sell more*). Use the Scaling Readiness Checklist (*Appendix I*) to determine if your business is prepared for growth.

Q: How do I decide whether to take on external funding or remain self-funded?

A: Consider:

- Self-funding retains complete control but limits scalability.
- External funding accelerates growth but may involve giving up equity or taking on debt. Refer to the Funding Decision Matrix in *Appendix I* to weigh pros and cons and check out the Capital raising journey in *Chapter 8: How to get all the funding you need*.

U.S.-Specific Challenges

Q: What tax advantages are available for small businesses?

A: Look for:

- Small Business Health Care Tax Credits for employers offering health insurance.
- Use the Tax Planning Basics template (*Appendix I*) to identify applicable deductions.

Q: What regulations or licenses are necessary for my business type?

A: Research industry-specific licenses at sba.gov. Use the Compliance Checklist (*Appendix I*) to meet state and federal requirements. Additionally, see *Appendix III and IV*, which have a legal checklist and Import/Export requirements, respectively.

Q: What are the tax implications of different business structures?

LLCs offer pass-through taxation, meaning profits flow directly to members' tax returns. C-Corps are taxed at both the corporate and shareholder levels (double taxation) but offer better venture capital access.

Many small businesses overpay taxes due to improper structuring, and choosing the wrong structure can result in excessive taxation, so consult with a CPA to choose the most tax-efficient entity. Use tools like TaxAct to simulate tax outcomes for various structures.

Q: Are there tax credits for startups?

The R&D tax credit is common. You may also qualify for state-specific grants. Consult with your CPA or visit the IRS website for more details.

Missing out on tax credits reduces available cash flow, so use tools like TaxPoint to track and apply for R&D and other tax credits. According to the IRS, many businesses underutilize the R&D tax credit due to a lack of awareness.

Inspiration and Resilience

Q: How can I stay motivated during challenging times?

A: Draw inspiration from military resilience principles Terry shared, such as:

- OODA Loop: Observe, Orient, Decide, Act—adapt quickly to changing circumstances (*Chapter 5: Are you ready to take the helm*).
- Commander's Intent: Focus on the end goal while being flexible with execution (*Chapter 1: The sounds of Dive, Dive, Dive*).

Share victories, no matter how small, with your team to maintain morale.

Q: How do I balance work and personal life while growing my business?

A: Tips (also covered in *Chapter 9: The Silent Shift – Turning Inward*) include:

- Set boundaries: Designate specific hours for work and personal time.
- Delegate: Trust your team to handle day-to-day operations.
- Use tools like the Goal Setting and Progress Tracker to prioritize effectively (See *Appendix I*).

Q: What are common mistakes new business owners make, and how can I avoid them?

A: Common pitfalls include:

- Underestimating costs: Use accurate budgeting tools like the Startup Budget Template.
- Avoiding delegation: Micro-managing limits growth.
- Failing to adapt: Use strategies like the OODA Loop to stay agile in changing markets.

Chapter 6: Why Businesses Fail provides a forensic assessment of pitfalls to avoid.

ACKNOWLEDGEMENTS AND CONTACT

T.I

As I mentioned in the dedication, there are two remarkable USN Submariners who defined excellence in both leadership and life:

My father, MMCM Wallace Gerald Ingram Sr., and ETCM Raymond Rudolph Kuhn Sr. (Life Mentor). Together, these two extraordinary men shaped not just my career but the very core of who I would become. One showed me the height of leadership through unfailing integrity, while the other taught me the power of steadfast compassion. This book has carried forward their legacy: The demanding excellence of two Master Chiefs who led with both mind and heart and the unwavering support of a mentor who knew when to be firm and when to show grace. I hope these pages have honored their impact, and may readers glimpse the remarkable influence of two men who understood that authentic leadership is about lifting others to heights they never thought possible. I want to thank a father who showed me what greatness looks like and a mentor who helped me pursue it. Your lessons still navigate me, so thank you!

The journey from a fledgling entrepreneur to a trusted advisor has been one marked by the extraordinary faith of others and the quiet sacrifices of those closest to my heart.

To my daughters - you have given up countless evenings, weekends, and precious moments together, often unwillingly but always with understanding

Depth and dividends

beyond your years. Your sacrifices were never unnoticed, even if business demands sometimes took precedence. Know that every late night, every missed event, every "just one more call" was in service not just to our family but to the many families whose lives we touched through our work. Your understanding has helped build something that extends far beyond us, touching lives and creating opportunities for others. You are my most outstanding achievement and my constant inspiration.

A special, heartfelt thank you to Roger Michaud (Retired), who wrote that very first order and took a chance on a passionate entrepreneur just starting out. Your belief in me laid the foundation for everything that followed.

To those early clients who saw beyond the size of our company to the depth of our commitment - your trust in those first crucial years gave us the opportunity to prove that dedication and results matter more than size and history. You bet on determination, and that bet has paid dividends for us all.

Over three decades, this trust has evolved into enduring partnerships. To our current clients who welcome us into their boardrooms, strategic sessions, and day-to-day operations - thank you for allowing us to "carry the water" alongside you. Your willingness to explore new heights, tackle complex challenges, and pursue extraordinary opportunities continues to inspire us. Together, we've proven that the best business relationships are built not just on services rendered but on a shared commitment to excellence.

To my partners and our team, who share this dedication to client success - your expertise and unwavering support make every achievement possible.

Each relationship, from that first order to our current partnerships and every sacrifice made by my family, has contributed to something greater than ourselves: the opportunity to impact lives, build futures, and create lasting value for generations to come.

With deepest gratitude,
Terry J. Ingram

DW

> *Have I not commanded you? Be strong and courageous. Do not be afraid, nor be dismayed, for the Lord your God is with you wherever you go.*
>
> **Joshua 1: 9.**

The Commander of Heavens Armies has kept me grounded and encouraged even during relentless battles, with words such as those above, since that 1st radical encounter I had, so glory to God in the Highest Heavens, and Peace on earth to those on whom his favor rests.

I am especially grateful to Mum for her indomitable entrepreneurial spirit, to my big brother Dennis, who was a great mentor, and to my big sister Doreen, who in many ways has always been my biggest cheerleader and business partner for all my wacky ideas.

Finally, I want to especially thank our five children for giving me an ultimate purpose for writing and to Brenda, a.ka Rabadob, my darling wife and "personal person" – love always xxx.

ABOUT THE AUTHORS

Terry J. Ingram is a globally recognized executive leader with over three decades of experience, beginning his journey in the USN Submarine Service and evolving into pivotal executive roles across marine, industrial, and commercial manufacturing sectors. As CEO and President of multiple corporations, he has led transformative projects for major global enterprises while successfully expanding operations throughout the Americas, Asia-Pacific, Europe, and UAE. A strategic visionary and hands-on leader, Ingram has consistently driven corporate growth through successful start-ups, second-stage growth, acquisitions, turnarounds, and international partnerships.

Dickson Wasake, FCCA, has 20+ years of experience in audit, accounting, and advisory with Big 4 (*PwC, Deloitte*) and Top 10 (*Baker Tilly*) global accounting practices. He is an ex-audit partner.

He has worked with Small and medium-sized businesses (SMBs) and listed multinationals, including one with $1.3 trillion of assets under management listed on the NYSE. His clients have included *World Bank/IDB* and *UN-funded projects, Coca-Cola and Unilever franchises, a Central Bank, an $800 billion asset manager, and a $1 billion blockchain* asset manager. Dickson is a poet and has written 7+ books and 50+ thought leadership articles.

www.ingramcontent.com/pod-product-compliance
Lightning Source LLC
Chambersburg PA
CBHW071022240526
45469CB00006BD/2052